If you are running a small business then you probably do not have the time for general, theoretical and often unnecessary details covered by many business and management books. But you do need advice which relates to your own working environment and this is now available in a practical, easy-to-follow format.

The NatWest Business Handbooks is a series of books written by authors with many years' experience and who are still actively involved in the day-to-day running of a small business.

These handbooks provide everything you need to tackle everyday issues and will enable you to:

• concentrate on specific areas which are particularly problematic to a small business

• adopt a step-by-step approach to the implementation of sound business skills

The author

Gary Jones is a lecturer in Business
Information Technology at Blackpool and The
Fylde College. He has lectured on numerous
small business courses, and advised and
worked on a number of projects for national
examining bodies. He also has considerable
business experience in retail management, run
his own small business, and is the author of
Running a Shop and *Marketing Decisions*.

*To my wife Doris for filling my life with love
and happiness*

& NatWest

BUSINESS
HANDBOOKS

*Small Books
with Big
Information*

starting up

third edition

Gary Jones

PITMAN
PUBLISHING

PITMAN PUBLISHING
128 Long Acre, London WC2E 9AN

A Division of Pearson Professional Limited

First published in Great Britain 1995
Second edition 1991
Third edition 1995

© Pearson Professional Limited 1995

British Library Cataloguing in Publication Data
A CIP catalogue record for this book can be obtained from the British
Library.

ISBN 0 273 61701 X

10 9 8 7 6 5 4 3

---

*The information in this book is intended as a general guide based upon the
legislation at the time of going to press. Neither the Bank, its staff nor the
author can accept liability for any loss arising as a result of reliance upon any
information contained herein and readers are strongly advised to obtain
professional advice on an individual basis.*

Typeset by Avocet Typeset, Brill, Aylesbury, Bucks
Printed and bound in Great Britain by Bell and Bain Ltd, Glasgow

The Publishers' policy is to use paper manufactured from sustainable forests.

contents

preface

Thinking about starting up in business?
Don't know where to start?
Confused by other books?

This book has been designed for you. It will help you understand and plan what hat to be done in plain and clear language.

Going into business is deceptively simple, staying in business and making a success of it is not – 1990 went on record as the worst year for a decade for small business failures. It is now 1995 and the much promised recovery is yet to be seen! However, many small business ventures are profitable and a few show remarkable growth. Success and failure are not the alternative results of the toss of a coin. Being in the right place at the right time is partly luck, but more to do with good planning. Many who enter the failure statistics simply did not plan. If you use this book intelligently you should not be one of them, for this book is about small business planning. The book will help you to:

- generate business ideas.
- weigh up the pros and cons of buying an existing business, franchise or starting from scratch.
- select an idea that stands a good chance of success.
- avoid the common mistakes that contribute to early business failure.
- lay out the framework for your business plan.
- identify the market for your business idea.
- refine the idea to match with what customers want.
- win customers and build sales.
- select the right type of premises.
- take steps to ensure the business makes sufficient profit.
- calculate the cash required to keep your business alive and well.

Guidelines are given to help you weigh up the pros and cons of partnerships, cooperatives and limited companies.

The book can be used in many ways. You can simply read it from cover to cover to give you a general understanding of what is involved, or work slowly through each chapter and section, building up your business plan as you proceed. You can, however, refer to each chapter in the order that suits you best. Further each chapter ends with a concise summary and most have detailed checklists to help you monitor your progress and as far as possible make sure you don't leave out a vital element in your preparations. The final chapter contains an overall pre-start-up checklist.

The book is based in part on my own personal experience of managing a number of businesses. I hope I have given you a practical, useable book that will guide you in the hard, interesting and, finally, personally and financially rewarding task in front of you.

Gary Jones
March 1995

Part 1

choosing your business

1

business ideas

Why start your own business?

Setting up in business for the first time or expanding an existing business can be an exciting experience. It can be the road to riches and personal fulfilment. It can also be the road to financial ruin and personal misery. Successful businesses are in the main the result of careful research and planning; enthusiasm, self-confidence and commitment, although essential, are not enough on their own.

Careful consideration should be given to the options for earning a livelihood. For most people the decision is between employment, unemployment and self-employment. What are the advantages and disadvantages of each? What's good about your present situation? What will you be giving up if you start your own business? What will you be gaining?

To help you weigh up the alternatives, consider the experiences of two people who recently started their own small businesses:

'... it's been good to get away from the petty bickering at work ... nobody breathing down your neck every minute of the day ... above all else, I enjoy taking the responsibility, making the decisions – when they have come off it has brought a great sense of achievement and sometimes relief – when they haven't, solving the problems has been a challenge ... being in business is about solving problems ... it was hard at first, the hours are still long but the business is doing well and I should be reaping the financial dividends by the end of next year...'

3

'... to begin with I expected to work hard; however, the pace hasn't slackened – in fact it's got worse – I find it difficult to keep track of all aspects of the business – you know, the accounts, letters, finding new customers, and there always seems to be problems with suppliers. I've had a lot of trouble finding enough cash to keep the business afloat – sales have not grown fast enough, but the bills keep coming in .,., the bank would not lend me any more money without a legal charge on my house – if the business fails I will lose everything. Sometimes the worry is too much. There have been many times when I've not been able to sleep at night. I've no family and social life any more – the business takes up too much time – one of the bad moments was six months ago, I was very ill with flu for two weeks. There was no way I could have stayed in bed – the business would have folded.'

➤ Take a sheet of paper and list about five advantages and five disadvantages of your present situation. Then do the same for a business venture you have in mind.

➤ How do the options balance out – is starting your own business the right alternative for you?

➤ What qualities do you think you need to succeed?

How can I find a 'good' business idea?

It is likely that you have already decided to some extent what business you would like to start. However, you may be at the stage where you would welcome the opportunity to run your own business but are not sure in which direction to go. The following sections will help you to generate more business ideas and consider them in relation to your own motivation, interest, needs, skills and resources.

There are a multitude of business opportunities to choose from, ranging from home-based ideas such as furniture repairs, dress and curtain-making or growing decorative plants, through offering standard services such as domestic cleaning, car repairs, painting and decorating, to running a shop, restaurant, rest home or hotel. Maybe you are considering something larger, presenting a more difficult challenge, such as manufacturing.

There are no 'magic formulas' for generating business ideas. However, the following activities will help you draw up a range, all of them proving more fruitful if you attempt them with a friend.

Building on your skills, hobbies or interests

➤ *Take five minutes to list as many of your interests and skills as you can think of. For each, try to think of a business idea to match it. For example:*

Interest/skills	*Business idea*
Hiking	Guided country walks
Cooking	Home catering; restaurant
Meeting people	Taxi proprietor; retailing

Having problems?

➤ *If you are struggling to find business ideas, use publications such as* Business Ideas *(available from W.H. Smith),* Exchange and Mart, *the classified section of your local paper, the* Yellow Pages *or British Telecom's* Business to Business *directory to make a list that appeals to you. Use it to identify any ideas that match up with your own skills or interests.*

Copying or improving somebody else's successful idea

It is a common fallacy that for a business to be a success it must be based on an innovative and original idea. In fact the opposite can be true: the less the idea has already been tried and tested by other entrepreneurs, the greater the element of risk.

➤ *Make a list of the businesses in your area that appear to be successful. Do any appeal to you?*

➤ *Can you improve on any already established businesses? For the existing businesses that appeal to you, try to make a list of the things that they do badly. How could you alter that business to improve on it?*

Combining two existing business ideas in a new way

An interesting activity is to attempt to combine two or more existing business ideas to produce a new concept. One well-known and highly successful example of this was the 'Body Shop'. The Body Shop offers mainly 'beauty products' made from 'natural ingredients without cruelty to animals'. It was started in 1976 with one shop; it is now a very successful business with shops worldwide. The Body Shop is basically a combination of the traditional herbalists with the cosmetic business, integrated in such a way as to capitalize on the recent trend towards healthier life-styles and public resentment and concern about 'cruelty to animals'.

➤ *Can you think of new ways to combine existing business ideas? It will help you to consider the needs of potential customers, through spotting a gap in the market – read on!*

Spotting a gap in the market

Many of today's successful business people have got where they have by identifying and exploiting a 'gap' in a fast-growing market. It is a matter of identifying needs of sections of the market which are presently not met by existing businesses. Richard Branson's Virgin Airlines established itself by meeting the need of a large section of the travelling public for cheap air travel. Club Eighteen to Thirty provides holidays for the under-thirties. A recent and more novel idea was the launch of a free newspaper for the 'rich', which provided a successful business for its originators by selling advertising space to manufacturers of 'quality' high-priced products.

Spotting a gap in the market is not necessarily easy Some suggestions for attempting this are as follows:

➤ *Try to identify current national and local trends. The HMSO publication Social Trends (found in the reference section of most public libraries) can be an invaluable source of such information, as can local and national newspapers, and TV newscasts and current affairs programmes such as* The Money Programme *(BBC2).*

➤ *Having identified what you think are a number of interesting trends, try to translate them into possible business ideas, by identifying a possible market need each suggests and a business idea that feasibly might meet that need. For example:*

Trend	Need	Possible business idea
Increase in crime against the person	Greater personal security	Home security services or products Personal security servie or products Self defences classes
Increase in single-parent families	Occasional freedom from pressure of looking after their children	Baby-sitting service Safe transport and supervision of children to and from school Setting up of town centre nursery to enable the parent to shop or go to work 'unhindered'

etc ....

➤ *Listen to what people say. Many times you will hear people say such things as ... 'if only ...*
   they stocked ...
   there was a cheap ...
   there was a decent bus service between ...
   you could rely on "them", I would pay to have "it" done ...
   they opened late I would use them more often ...'

*If enough people say the same thing there **might** be a gap in the market.*

Of course you would have to research whether any market need or gap you discover is already sufficiently met in your area. As with all initial business ideas, proceed with caution. Do not assume too much from limited information

Is it a good idea?

I hope the preceding activities have enabled you to compile a list of possible business ideas for you to explore. At some stage you must decide on which idea to investigate further. The factors that affect your final choice from a short list of potential business ideas can be split broadly into personal and business considerations.

Personal considerations

Your skills – can you do it?

When starting a business, many people wish to capitalize on existing skills. If this is an important consideration for you, carefully consider each business idea on your list in relation to your skills.

Perhaps you do not consider this an important factor. New skills and knowledge can be obtained by a number of means. Your local further education college or adult education centre will probably be able to offer you a course in your area of need. Alternatively, or in support of joining a course, you may be able to seek temporary employment in a business of your choice, gaining the skills and knowledge first-hand.

Your interests

An important question to ask yourself is, 'will I like the "work" the business involves?' There is little point in establishing a business that involves a considerable amount of work that you don't enjoy or even detest. For each of your possible business ideas try and identify what daily work activities it will involve. If you don't know, find out; again by taking temporary or part-time work in that area or if that is not possible by talking to and observing people in that type of business.

Your personal commitments

It is important to have the support of your family and friends. Are they prepared to put up with you spending evenings and weekends helping your business grow! If not, look for a less demanding form of business.

Business considerations

Is there a market for your product or service?

This is of paramount importance. Without a sufficient market for your product or service, your business is doomed before it starts. Chapter 3 deals in detail with market research but initially you must be able to answer roughly some of the following basic questions in relation to your selected business ideas:

- who will buy your product or service?
- why will they buy from you instead of the competition?
- how big is the market?
- what will your share be?
- is the market over-supplied?
- is the market growing or contracting?

How much capital will the business require – can you afford it?

This is obviously an important consideration. Chapter 7 will help you calculate the amount you will require to start the business. Chapter 8 will tell where you can obtain finance and how to go about raising it. As a rough guide, most financial institutions will require you to put up nearly half the total requirement of the business venture. As regards what it will cost (see Chapter 6), service businesses tend to be cheaper to set up than those involving specialized premises and expensive equipment.

At this stage it is important to have a clear idea of the amount of personal capital you can raise.

➤ *Make a list of your assets.*

Assets	Cash value
House value	How much personal capital do you have tied up in your house? Make a conservative estimate of the market value of your house and subtract the balance of your mortgage outstanding. Note: you can remortgage your house usually up to 80% of its valuation
Life assurance policies	You can obtain a quote on their current surrender value. *Whether this is a sensible financial decision needs careful consideration*
Material possessions	For instance, you may have a new car that you can sell and replace with a cheaper second-hand one

Choosing your business

Shares

Premium bonds   Cash value

Savings accounts

Coming to a final decision is a matter of weighing all the above considerations. It will help you to have some objective method of bringing them all together. Choosing a business is similar to choosing a house. Try the following:

➤ *Make a list of what you require from a business venture. This might include items such as:*

- regular hours
- flexible hours
- no unsocial hours
- high degree of profits
- low capital requirements
- no need to employ people
- does not involve personal selling
- meeting people
- little paperwork
- will exploit existing skills
- involves working outdoors
- will provide potential for expansion
- involves travelling
- involves working from home
- will not require expensive premises
- involves little risk

➤ *Consider your list and decide which are the most important and least important requirements. To make it clearer give each requirement a weighting to signify how important it is, for instance from 1 to 10 (the more important the requirement is, the higher the weighting).*

To illustrate this method take the example of Ann, who had two young children at school and little capital. She wanted to run a small business that would give her sufficient income, but more important she wanted to gain a sense of achievement and fulfilment from what she did. She also wanted to meet people and 'broaden her horizons'. She had some skills in sewing and claimed to have an eye for fashion, having made some of her children's clothes which had drawn favourable comment from her friends.

Ann's list of requirements for a business venture looked like this:

Requirement	Importance
Low capital required (below £2500)	10
Flexible hours	9
Able to work from home	4
Interest/satisfaction	7
Able to meet people	9

Low capital was very important because of the small amount she could raise. As Ann had to take to, and pick up her children from school, having decided that the cost of a child minder would be too great, flexible hours or hours that coincided with school hours was also an important consideration.

Ann had drawn up a short list of three business ideas:

1. Producing soft toys for sale on a rented stall in the local market.
2. Buying and selling children's wear via a party plan.
3. Alterations on contract with local fashion shops.

➤ *The next step is to score each of your business ideas against the weighted requirements. Award points to each business idea from 0 to 10 – high points if it meets the requirement well, low if it does not. Give each business idea a score, marking its success in meeting each requirement by multiplying the points awarded by the importance factor. The overall score is obtained by adding together the scores for each business idea.*

Ann's ideas fared as follows:

Requirement	Importance	Soft toys		Children's party plan		Alterations	
		Points	Score	Points	Score	Points	Score
Low capital required							
(below £2500)	10	3	30	10	100	5	50
Flexible hours	9	2	18	8	72	10	90
Able to work from home	4	4	16	8	32	8	32
Interest/ satisfaction	7	5	35	8	56	4	28
Able to meet people	9	7	63	9	81	3	27
			162		341		227
Total possible score			390		390		390
Percentage of total score possible			41.5%		87%		58%

In the example, the party plan idea appears to be best suited to Ann – scoring the highest and meeting 87% of her requirements. As a guide, your highest scoring business must meet well in excess of 50% of your requirements. If it does not, it is suggested that you examine other options or reassess your evaluations of each business.

A note of warning: although this method is useful for ordering your thoughts to help you make a decision, your results will only be as accurate as your evaluations. The method will help ensure that your business is well matched to your personal requirements – it does not tell you whether the business will be a success.

Checklist

- Have you the health and stamina for your selected venture?
- Can you cope with the stresses and strains?
- Are you prepared to take a calculated risk?
- How will you cope if the going gets tough both in the

planning and running of the business?
- We all have strengths and weaknesses – what are yours?
- How are you going to exploit your strong points?
- What are you going to do about your weak points?
- Have you the necessary skills?
- Are you a self-starter?
- Do you have self-discipline?
- Can you work long hours over a sustained period?
- Have you discussed your project with your family and friends?
- Do you have their support?
- Have you thought long and hard and identified your reasons for going into business?
- Have you discussed your responses to this checklist with somebody who knows you well?

Should I buy an existing business?

Having decided to go into business and selected a potential business idea the question arises, should I start from scratch or buy an existing business? If you are one of the few who have a completely new product or service, the decision, by definition, is made for you. For others, the choice is open.

A major appeal of buying an existing business is speed – the business is a *going concern* – hopefully, revenue will come in from day one. There is little inconvenience: no looking for suitable premises, choosing equipment or finding new customers and suppliers.

A second and important advantage is that if you have selected your business well, you will have a sound base from which to expand, innovate and perhaps change direction. Starting from scratch, it often takes three to six months to reach a viable sales level. An existing business will have a track record. You can look at past sales records and have an accountant check out its financial viability. When starting from scratch, the risk is greater; market research can provide good estimates of potential revenue – but it cannot guarantee it!

There are disadvantages, however. Starting from scratch can be cheaper, as you are not paying for *goodwill*. Also, you can often more easily obtain exactly what you require in terms of premises, location, equipment and so on. Buying a business is sometimes like buying a second-hand car or house – there are unseen flaws. After you take over, you may find that the premises are not really as suitable as you thought – they might be in the wrong place, have the wrong equipment and there may be not sufficient room for expansion, e.g. planning permission cannot be gained for an extension.

Buyers new to business often make the mistake of relying too heavily on the past accounts of the business for assurance that it is a viable concern. 'Let the buyer beware' is a saying worth remembering. The problem with records is two-fold.

First, the records refer to what has happened *in the past* – there is no guarantee that the business will continue to be a success in the future. For instance, the previous owner's business may have been based on personal reputation – when he goes so does the business. I know of a young couple who recently purchased a small hotel, the accounts of which showed good past trade. The previous owner purchased another hotel in the same vicinity and took his regular clientele with him. The young couple are now in the position of having to build up their clientele from scratch and as a consequence have serious cash-flow problems.

Secondly, accounts can conceal as much as they reveal, and depend for their accuracy on the honesty of the owner of the business. It should also be noted that the accounts do not give the full story. For instance, they do not tell you whether double yellow lines are going to be placed outside your newly acquired newsagent's shop or about the large store that is going to open up close by and take away all your trade.

Whether you decide to buy or start from scratch, the detailed research and planning that this book deals with is equally applicable to both forms of business start-up.

Checklist – buying an existing business

1. How long would it take to start this business from scratch?
2. What is the cost of starting from scratch?
3. What degree of risk is there in starting from scratch?
4. Why buy an existing business?

5. Look at a range of businesses, go to your local commercial estate agent.
6. How many properties would you look at before making a decision to buy a house?
7. Have you 'viewed' at least this many businesses?
8. Will the vendor provide you with copies of at least three years' accounts?
9. If not, lose interest immediately!
10. What degree of certainty is there that you will retain the business's customers once the present owners depart?
11. Have you deciphered the real reasons for the sale? Don't take the vendor's reasons at face value!
12. What present and future threats and opportunities are there to the business (see Chapter 2).
13. What *exactly* is included in the sale?
14. What is the sales trend (over at least the past three years)?
15. When you subtract inflation from these figures what does the real trend look like?
16. In relation to present and future customers (see Chapter 3) what is a conservative estimate of its future potential?
17. Compare these sales figures to trends in this sector of business. For example, an increase of 10% in sales when the market has increased by 30% in the same period means the business is contracting not expanding!
18. What is the net profit now, is it enough for both:
    a) personal requirements?
    b) re-investment in the business to enable it to grow?
19. What is the real trend in profits? Look out for unusually high closing stocks – these can artificially push up the profit figure (see Chapter 6).
20. Calculate the net profit as a percentage of the total investment in the business (see Chapters 6 and 7).
21. How many years will the business take to pay for itself? (Note, as a rough guide, the business should pay for itself in less than five years.)
22. Have you examined all the overheads?
23. Are they realistic?
24. If stock is included:
    will the stock sell?
    how has it been valued?

is it a realistic valuation?

25. What is the value of the business's net assets (see Chapter 7)?
26. How does this compare to the asking price?
27. How many years at current profit levels will it take you to cover the asking price?
28. What value, if any, has been placed on 'goodwill'?
29. What was your answer to point 10?
30. What is the ceiling price you are not prepared to exceed?
31. Are there any hidden costs to the purchase (e.g. redecoration costs, replacement of unsuitable equipment)?
32. What points are there for negotiation with the vendor?
33. Can the asking price be brought down?
34. Refer to and apply the 'premises checklist' at the end of Chapter 5.

What is a franchise – is it a good way to start?

An increasingly popular alternative to starting from scratch or buying an existing business is to buy a franchise. A franchise is a business relationship between a franchisor (owner of a name or method of business) and a franchisee (a local operator of that business). The franchisee agrees to pay the franchisor a certain sum of money for use of the business name or method of doing business or both, usually in the form of an initial fee and some agreed percentage of sales or similar.

The main advantage of starting a business by becoming a franchisee is that you are usually buying a tried and tested method for doing a particular business. Consequently, there should be a greater chance of success than with buying an existing business or starting from scratch.

The franchisor will dictate to varying degrees how the business should be run. Often this will include instructing and advising the franchisee on the product or service range, pricing policy, size and design of premises and sometimes even the style of uniform the employees should wear. A good franchisor will also provide a back-up service giving advice where applicable on such aspects as management, training, merchandising, accounts, etc. Larger franchisors will usually offer advertising and sales promotion support.

The size of franchise businesses varies considerably. The initial cost of buying a franchise ranges from a few thousand upwards to half a million pounds. Franchising has now become so popular (there are now in excess of 18,000 franchises in the UK) that most of the major clearing banks have set up specialist sections to deal with finance applications from potential franchisees.

The main disadvantage of becoming a franchisee is that the business is never truly yours. As the franchisor lays down certain requirements, which can be quite comprehensive, you can never run the business exactly as you want. If the franchisor is not flexible enough to take into account the changing nature of your local business environment, this lack of control can have adverse effects on your business. Finally, you will never be able to keep all of your profits, as most franchise agreements involve some form of continuing payment to the franchisor related to sales or profits.

Taking up a franchise can be an attractive starting point for those entering into business for the first time. But beware: not all franchise operations are the same. As a guide to investigating a franchise, use the checklist below. If the franchise is worth purchasing, you must receive satisfactory answers to each question on the checklist.

Checklist – Taking up a franchise

The franchise operation and operator

1. How long has the franchisor been operating in the UK?
2. How many outlets are in operation? How many have closed and why?
3. Are the present outlets successful? Does the franchise have a good name with its customers and operators?
4. Will this type of business be successful in your area? Is there a viable market in your area?
5. What is the competition in your area?
6. Is the franchise operating in an expanding or contracting market? Is it keeping pace with changes in the market?
7. Is the franchisor a member of the British Franchise Association?
8. What is the financial position of the franchisor? Obtain a copy of the audited accounts.

9. Will the franchisor allow you to take up references on him?

The franchise agreement

1. What is the initial payment – what does it entitle you to?
2. What will your liability be for the payment of royalties?
3. On what conditions can/will the franchise be terminated?
4. What will the franchisor contract to provide?
5. Are there minimum sales figures to be met?

Finance

The clearing banks have recognized the importance of franchising as a means of helping individuals to become independent business people. It is not very often that individuals will have cash available to finance their investment in a chosen franchise and many would argue that it would be better for franchisees to take on some level of debt, which will have to be serviced as a result of their efforts.

In ordinary business start-ups, it is not uncommon for assistance from the lender to be limited to 50% of start-up costs. This reflects the uncertainties associated with new ventures, in particular with regard to potential demand, revenue forecasts, etc.

In the case of a proven business format franchise, however, many of these uncertainties are removed because the system has been shown to work. That being so, the level of assistance from a bank in relation to the proprietor's involvement can often justifiably be increased, perhaps to a maximum ratio of 2:1, also with possible reduction in security needed. Borrowing in excess of these guidelines produces a heavy burden on profits in the form of interest payments. Experience shows that the business is then greatly disadvantaged from the outset.

Generally speaking therefore your research should be confined to franchises where the total level of investment required is not more than three times the cash you put in, i.e. the amount of borrowed money is not more than twice the cash input. In this respect, full start-up costs should be gauged as accurately as possible. Often franchisors' prospectuses only list basic costs.

Financial projections provided by franchisors should be

checked independently, by an accountant. The basis on which they have been produced should be established. Any cash flow projections (see Chapter 7) should take into account the cost of any bank borrowing and loan repayments in addition to the franchisee's personal expenditure requirements.

The loan facilities agreed are most commonly taken in the form of specifically structured loans with additional overdraft facilities for working capital purposes. The loans may include such features as fixed monthly repayments and fixed interest rates to ease budgeting, plus a capital repayment holiday in the early stages of the business's development.

In those cases where the proposition does not measure up to the banks' normal criteria and personal assets have been pledged, then the banks may be prepared to assist under the Small Firms Loan Guarantee Scheme, provided they are satisfied with the underlying viability of the venture. Here the bank can lend up to a maximum amount (currently £100000) against a guarantee from the government covering up to 70 per cent of the amount borrowed at preferential rates (currently 2.5% over Base Rate). There is a premium payable to cover the provision of the guarantee (currently 2.5% per annum) as an additional cost to the borrower.

Special finance schemes may have been agreed by the banks with specific franchisors and these will usually apply where the fran-chisor company has a good track record in franchising, its finan-cial position is sound and its management capability is strong.

Further information on franchises can be obtained from The British Franchise Association, Franchise Chambers, Thames View, Newton Road, Henley-on-Thames, Oxon RG9 1HG; tel. 01491 578049. The Association produces a package advising on all aspects of purchasing and operating a franchise, including a list of all franchisors registered with the Association. The fee for the package is currently only a few pounds and is obtainable at the above address by return post.

Summary

If you didn't have a business idea before you started this chapter, I hope the activities have helped you to generate some new and interesting ones for further consideration. If you already had a good idea about what you would like to do, some of the other activities should have made you pause for thought and make sure that the idea matches your personal requirements and resources. The rest of the book is about researching and planning the business venture in more detail. The next chapter will introduce you to the importance of planning, the mistakes that many new businesses make, and help you to get organized for the interesting and demanding task ahead.

2
the plan of action

Why do so many new businesses fail? • *Making a start at the planning process – problems and constraints* • *Checklist – Preparing planning guidelines* • *What are the threats and opportunities to the idea?* • *The completed plan* • *Summary*

This chapter discusses some of the common mistakes made by small business people and, in doing so, emphasizes the importance of completing a detailed business plan before opening for business. You will also be given a framework around which you can build your business plan; the detail can be added to the framework as you work through the second part of the book. Much emphasis is placed on looking to the future, with the aim of spotting both threats and opportunities. The aim is to make sure you will always survive in times of recession and grow in times of boom.

Why do so many new businesses fail?

Sales and profits have been squeezed and many more small businesses have entered the failure statistics. However, business failures cannot be blamed solely on the ups and downs of the economy. Even in 'good years' thousands of businesses will fail. The real problem is that far too many small businesses don't bother to take the trouble to undertake serious and effective business planning. Good business planning enables growth and increased profitability in times of boom and ensures survival in the lean years.

The pity is that most people will plan their holidays but not their business. Would you set out on your holidays not knowing where you were going, what route or transport to take, how much it will cost to get there, whether there will be accommodation at the end of your journey and how long you will spend at each place? Perhaps such a holiday may appeal to the wildly adventurous – but would you go into business in this way? It sounds absurd, but many small

21

business people proceed exactly like this, muddling through from one day to the next. The 'adventure' usually ends in bankruptcy and in some of the worst cases prison for fraudulent trading.

We can begin to understand what a good business plan should be about by examining the mistakes people make. These can be categorized under the general headings:

Marketing
Finance and investment
Organization and control

Marketing

Trying to sell what nobody wants to buy

This is just one of the symptoms resulting from lack of knowledge about the business's market. Marketing research is essential if you are to avoid this basic sin. As you will discover in the next chapter, marketing is about developing a product and service that customers want to buy, rather than a product you want to sell. Too many start with the product first and then attempt to find customers. This is definitely putting the cart before the horse!

Insufficient sales

This is part of the same problem. Many enter into business with no valid and reliable projection of first year's sales. Without such a projection it is impossible to know:

- what scale of operation you should commit yourself to
- how much cash you will need, and when, to keep your business alive
- what profits you will make

It's like taking a job without asking what you will be paid, then hoping for the best!

Overemphasis on price

Many small businesses believe that price is all important and end up underpricing their product or service. This blinkers the business to other, often more important, customer-buying motives. For instance, a property repair business attempting to sell on price when its customers consider quality, reliability and speed of service as being more important, will not capture much business.

Right product, right price, wrong place

Finding the best route to your customers is vitally important. Many businesses have a product at a price that customers want. The problem? – they are selling it through the wrong intermediaries or by the wrong method or in the wrong place. Your customers will not beat a path to your door simply because you have the right product at the right price. Your customer's decision to buy is influenced just as much by such factors as convenience, accessibility, and image of the place from which the product/service is sold.

Do not be tempted, as many other small business people have been, to take premises because the rent, rates or purchase price is low or simply because you like the area.

Finance and investment

Mistaking cash for profit

One of the commonest errors is to mistake cash for profit. Cash and profit are two distinct items. Cash can come from a variety of sources: loans, overdrafts, retained profits, etc. Profits come from the difference between a business's revenue and its costs. Profit can be tied up in stocks and equipment and not necessarily in the form of a growing bank balance. For instance, a business can be making a profit but be overdrawn at the bank because all of its cash is tied up in stock and debtors (people who owe it money). This position is fine if it is controlled, planned for and temporary – it is when this becomes uncontrolled, not planned for and permanent that disaster strikes. Cash is the life blood of a business and without it raw materials, wages, stock, etc., cannot be purchased.

Underestimating the investment required

Far too many businesses fail to recognize the length of time it takes to get off the ground. This can vary from three to six months, and even longer with manufacturing businesses. In such cases, the scale of investment required in working capital (cash reserves, stocks, sales made on credit) to keep the business afloat is often overlooked.

Full costs of starting up and operating not identified

Many people start up in business without fully realizing the size and nature of the hidden costs involved. Often, extravagant purchases are made or certain items purchased outright which would have been better leased. All potential costs should be fully researched and alternative methods of financing considered.

Organization and control

No systems or policy for selecting, training and managing staff

Few who enter small business for the first time have had experience of selecting, employing and managing staff. Therefore, it is hardly surprising to find that many small businesses make costly mistakes in this area. One dishonest or poorly trained employee can cost you all of your profits.

Failure to keep records

Ask any small business person such questions as how this month's sales figures compare with last month's or how much profit was made this month and the likelihood is that the majority would not be able to give you an accurate answer. They either have not kept up to date with their records or don't have a proper and useful administration system. A business founded and operated on this basis has little chance of success. Without basic accounting information your business could be nearing failure without you recognizing it. You may miss the opportunity to take corrective action.

Making a start at the planning process – problems and constraints

The problem

Well, what have we learnt from other people's mistakes? First, that business survival and growth – the universal broad aims of all business – are dependent on two key factors:

CASH RESOURCES and LONG-TERM PROFITABILITY

Secondly, that these two pillars of business can only stem from healthy sales activity. Marketing is therefore in the centre stage. However, just as sales generate profit and cash they will also soak it up As they say, '*you don't get something for nothing*' (see Fig. 2.1).

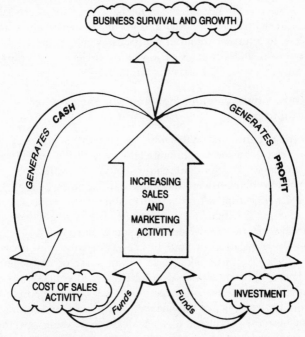

Fig. 2.1 The business cycle

The problem is to maintain a balance between investment and costs on the one hand and cash and profit generation on the other. Marketing objectives will drive you to invest and expand while financial objectives will pressurize you to prune and cut back. A good business plan should find the middle road that will lead to planned and steady growth. Overemphasizing the importance of either financial or marketing objectives can usher in disaster.

Over-zealous pursuit of sales targets can lead you to an 'over-trading' position. This is where investment in increasing sales (i.e. product development, additional customer services, more advertising, promotional events and so) takes out more cash than is being generated, to such an extent that the business becomes insolvent.

Equally so, low investment targets can lead to strangulation of the new business at birth. Particularly in times of recession, many businesses seem to catch the commercial equivalent of anorexia. As costs and investment are cut to the bone sales falter; further cuts are made, so sales contract further; less cash and profit are generated, which leads to a further round of cut backs, which in turn leads to less cash and profit. So the vicious circle continues until bankruptcy finally buries the business.

Know where you are, then you can decide where you want to be

Setting clear and achievable objectives is the key to successful business planning. However, this is easier said than done. To begin with you will have more questions and problems than answers and solutions. The best way to tackle objective setting is to map out in some detail your present situation. The logic is that you must identify first where you are before you can decide where you want to be.

The translation of your business idea to a fully fledged business plan will take place within a set of constraints. There will be constraints you have imposed yourself, say to minimize risk, and constraints that have been imposed on you, for example, by the finance you can raise, the nature of the business you intend to start, local competition, customer preferences and so on. All such factors will limit what you can feasibly do and therefore will provide overall limits to your objectives and, as such, guidelines for more detailed planning. Use the following guidelines to define in some detail the constraints you face. Some you may well be able to answer now, whilst others will have to wait until you have gathered more detailed information. Nonetheless, you will have made a start.

Checklist – preparing planning guidelines

Financial constraints

1. How much personal capital have you at your disposal?
2. How much can you raise in the form of loans?
3. Are you prepared to seek out partners or venture capital?

Constraints relating to personal and risk factors

1. How much do you need to take out of the business for your own personal needs?
2. How many hours are you prepared to work in any week?
3. Are you prepared to work unsocial hours?
4. Do you or your family object to living on the premises?
5. How much can you afford or are prepared to lose if the business fails?
6. Will you sacrifice a degree of security to obtain rapid growth?
7. Will you minimize risk by buying an existing business, franchise or start from scratch?
8. What degree of certainty will you require before you decide to start up?
9. Will you want to employ and manage staff or just keep the business as a one person or family operation?
10. Do you have your family's support?

Marketing constraints

1. Is there a good market for the product or service?
2. What is the minimum, as indicated by competitors, you will have to offer your customers in terms of product/service quality, range, availability, price and additional services to trade successfully?
3. Is demand for the product or service steady or is it subject to ups and downs?
4. Is the market growing or contracting?
5. Are the customers in the market easy or difficult to reach and sell to?
6. Will you have to purchase an existing business or franchise to enter the business selected?
7. How much competition is there?
8. What do the competition offer the customer?
9. Will price levels in the market allow you to trade profitably?

What are the threats and opportunities to the idea?

In identifying the constraints of your plan you will have largely determined what you will or can do and what you won't or can't do. The next step is to identify the strengths and weaknesses of your venture in relation to the threats and opportunities posed by the environment in which it will operate. From such an analysis you will be well placed to set detailed objectives with the aim of minimizing risk and maximizing opportunity.

The wider business environment is made up of the larger influences of the economy, social trends, population characteristics, laws (present and pending) and developments in technology. These factors, over which you will have little or no control, will directly or indirectly impinge on your day to day environment of competing with other businesses, increasing sales, dealing with suppliers and exploiting your business to the full.

The following guidelines will help you identify the threats and opportunities you face.

Economic factors

Interest rates

1. By intelligent reading of the quality press, viewing of the more in depth news programmes such as the *Money Programme, News Night and Channel 4 News*, what is likely to happen to interest rates over the next 12 months?
2. How sensitive are your markets to fluctuations in the rate of interest?
3. What percentage of your customers will buy using credit cards, credit sale agreements, bank loans and other forms of finance. Use *Social Trends* (HMSO), available at your local library, to find out.
4. What effect will 1, 2, 3, 4 and 5% changes in interest rates have on your financial targets?

Inflation

Prices of all products and services do not go up at the same rate. The various rates of inflation for the different types of products/services you sell and the goods and services your business consumes should be examined for their impact on costs, profits and sales. For example, a high rate of inflation on a product or service where price is an important factor can dramatically curtail sales. Further, if the prices of major items of cost are rising at a greater rate than the price of the items you sell then profits will be eroded.

1. Can increased costs caused by increases in the rate of inflation be passed on to your customers without a marked effect on sales?
2. Is your market(s) price sensitive? (more about this subject in Chapters 3 and 4).
3. In the type of business you are planning to enter, in the past have marked increases in the rate of inflation led to:
   - a uniform increase in the market price?
   - a price war with the competition?
   - increased competition on some other basis such as offering 0% finance, additional services, improved product quality, etc.?

Economic stability

You should examine the local economies that affect your markets. How prosperous are they? Are they stable, growing or in decline? Such general influences will have some overall impact on the market(s) you serve. Trends in unemployment rates are certainly indicators. Also, if your customers depend on a few large employers for their livelihood find out how well they are doing and if possible what their future plans are. For instance, a whole town can be decimated by just one large employer shifting production elsewhere.

If your customers are solely other businesses do not be misled into thinking that the stability and prosperity of consumer markets do not matter. After all they, like all businesses, ultimately depend on the consumer for success. Your principal client may not be selling direct to the consumer but the customers they do business with or, failing that the next business down the chain of distribution, will be. The effects of a depression in consumer markets will always filter down the chain of distribution from retailer, through intermediaries to the manufacturer and eventually to their suppliers. Sometimes the delay can be measured in terms of weeks and in others in terms of months or even years, as can be the case with engineering businesses making major production process equipment. Of course, the opposite is true when the economy booms – suppliers of plant and equipment to manufacturers will be the last to benefit.

1. What is the current unemployment rate amongst your customer groups?
2. Who employs your customers?
3. What is the state of their (your customers' employers) financial health?
4. What are the plans of your customers' employers?
5. Are any new employers planning to come into the area? (contact the Planning Department of your local authority and review the local press).
6. If your customers are other businesses then it is essential that you check their financial standing. You must watch their markets and marketing closely, after all you depend on them for success.
7. What is the time lag between boom and slump in your sector and boom and slump in relevant consumer markets?
8. What is the scale of the knock-on effect of boom and slump in consumer markets?

Changes in disposable income

Changes in real disposable income (i.e. after discounting the effect of inflation and taking into account taxation) can have a more dramatic effect on some markets than others. To illustrate, between 1981 and 1986 real disposable income rose by 17%. The most notable effects on sales to consumers were increases in clothes (up by 34%) and the purchases of TVs, etc. (up by a colossal 97%), whereas the spending on basic needs such as food remained fairly static.

Is there any correlation between disposable income and sales in the market you will enter?

Political and legal factors

1. Will changes in legislation in any of the following areas affect your business?
   – product design/safety
   – product description labelling and packaging
   – product guarantees
   – trade practices and regulatory bodies

- retail trading hours
- pricing
- advertising practice

2. Identify the consumer pressure groups that influence your markets. What are their present concerns? What degree of influence do they have on your business's target markets?
3. What plans for new housing, commercial, road transport and other developments are in the pipeline that may affect your markets and/or product distribution.
4. What subsidies, grants and guidance are available either to you or your competitors?

Population and social factors

The population of the UK has remained fairly static at around 56 million, projected to increase to only 60 million by the year 2025. This, however, masks major changes in the age, sex, economic activity and geographical distribution of the population. For example, a dip in the birth rate in the late 1970s has led to a 25 to 30% reduction in the number of school leavers in the early 1990s. As a direct result you would expect the suppliers of educational equipment to suffer, but the same demographic trend will present opportunities for others. For example, the contraction in the youth labour market will encourage women to return to work. The potential result, particularly if the government via legislation provides the right financial incentives, is a vast growth in the demand for nursery places.

Scrutinize population trends as they affect your markets. To do this, if relevant, you will need to have demographic features (e.g., age, sex, location, etc.) of your market included in your customer profile(s). For guidelines on how to construct customer profiles see Chapter 3.

The ideas and values of a society will affect to some degree the actions of all individuals within a social group. They are therefore of concern to all businesses. The trouble is they can be very difficult to pin down and define. Nonetheless some attempt must be made. Advertisers can make very effective use of changes in mass attitudes and values. Note how effectively the most unlikely businesses have turned 'green'.

1. What do you know about your customers' concerns, motivations and attitudes?
2. Are any of the following important factors?

31

- environmental concerns
- ethnic or local customs and traditions
- religious concerns
- life-style aspirations and expectations

Technological factors and change

Developments in technology have enabled businesses to create vast new markets, as has been the case with microwaves, home computers, small business micros, satellite television, compact disc players, and so on. It can also change fundamentally the way the business operates. For example, the advent of electronic point of sale equipment and bar code scanning in the retail industry has meant improved customer service and a reduction in operating costs. The same is the case in other industries. New technology has allowed the businesses that can afford the investment in equipment, personnel and training to introduce new production and distribution methods.

1. What has been the pattern of change in your type of business over the past 10 years?
2. Has change been rapid or slow – is this a trend that is likely to continue in the future?
3. Which companies have consistently led the way in product and market innovation – what can you learn from them?
4. Will you be able to make the same investment in change as your competitors?
5. Can you detect early enough the impact that technological changes might have on your production, distribution and marketing plans?

The completed plan

If you have thought about your business idea long and hard, and have done some initial research as indicated in the guidelines, you will have prepared the ground for building a detailed plan of action. Although the completed business plan is still a distant goal, it will nevertheless help to map out what has to be achieved. Working through the rest of this book will help you in this quest.

Your business plan (we will consider how it should be formally laid out for a loan application in Chapter 8) can be subdivided in many ways but it must cover the following areas.

Sales and marketing

Quite simply, no customers means no business! This simple truth means that you must define your business idea:

● in terms of the customers it will serve
● why customers will buy from you rather than the competition

You need to collect as much information as possible about the market for your business. Some of the key questions have already been posed in this chapter and the whole area will be considered in detail in the next two chapters.

The size and demands of your potential market and the activity of your competitors will lay down the parameters for decision-making relating to:

● scale of operation
● location and distribution
● the competition
● sales targets
● pricing and overall trading policy
● products and services
● additional customer services that need to be offered
● advertising and sales promotion policies

In summary, as a small business cannot significantly influence and change the nature of the market, you should evolve your overall business idea in response to the threats and opportunities posed by it.

Costs

This area of the plan will detail all the costs faced in starting and operating the business for at least the first year's trading. Here care should be taken not to mistake all business expenditure as cost. Costs relate only to expenditure on those items that are used up in a given period of trading, such as stock sold, wages, electricity, rent, rates, insurance and so on. Expenditure on items often associated with start-up such as equipment and premises is not a cost, they are something you are likely to still have at the end of the trading period and are called *assets*. As each year goes by some assets will lose value through ageing and wear and tear. The loss in value is a cost and is known as depreciation.

Some costs such as electricity, rent and rates do not change in proportion to how much you sell and are known as *fixed costs* or more commonly as *overheads*. Other costs, most significantly stock, vary in direct proportion with the amount you sell and are known as *variable* or *direct costs*.

A detailed investigation into the full costs of operating the business cannot be made until decisions relating to the scale and location of the operation (derived in part from market research and financial constraints) are made. However, identification of suppliers can begin almost immediately.

The formulation of objectives in this area are inextricably linked with sales targets and investment decisions.

You need to itemize and justify all costs.

Profit

This aspect of your planning will provide one of the acid tests for your sales and cost objectives. Will your sales bring in sufficient revenue to cover all costs and provide you with an 'acceptable profit'?

You will earn profit from the production or buying of merchandise or services and selling them. The difference between the direct or variable costs and the selling price is your *gross profit* which will have to contribute to payment of your overheads. What's left over is your *net profit*.

There are a number of factors that affect total profitability:

- sales volume
- price
- overheads or fixed costs
- gross profit margin

The term 'margin' needs to be explained. It is the percentage difference between direct costs and sales price. If I sell a machine for £50000 which cost £20000 to make, my total gross profit is £30000. The gross profit margin is 60%.

$$\frac{50\,000-20\,000}{50\,000} \times 100 = 60\%$$

Do not make the mistake of assuming that a high gross profit margin will bring high total gross profit. It's the number of times you earn that profit margin which determines the total gross profit earned at the end of the day.

When you have brought together your estimates of costs and revenue it is likely you will have to make at least minor adjustments to your sales and cost objectives. In fact the establishment of your sales, cost and profit plans, because they are so closely related, will take place hand in hand.

The key financial projections in this area are:

● *Break-even calculation* – this is the calculation of the sales level required to cover all costs, both fixed and variable. One important question to answer is: 'How long will it take for the business to break even?'

● *Projected profit and loss account* – this projection will give the expected position on sales, costs and profits at the end of the first year's trading.

Investment and finance

The amount of money you will have to invest in the assets of the business will be determined primarily by:

● the scale of operation
● whether you intend to buy freehold or leasehold
● the stock levels you will have to carry
● the level of credit sales

Any increase in the scale of the operation, the level of credit sales, and a decision to buy freehold will *increase* your investment in the business. Any decision to rent, or lease instead of buying major items of equipment ranging from vans to electronic tills, will *reduce* your investment.

Further, most businesses experience peaks and troughs in the amount of money going out (e.g. due to quarterly bills all coming at the same time) and coming in (e.g. due to seasonal fluctuations in sales). Therefore, at times there will be more money going out than coming in. This is fine over a short period of time – but over the long term you must plan your business so that a cash surplus position is reached. Full instruction, discussion and advice on cash flow forecasting and control is given in Chapter 7.

Finally, the rate of return on the money invested in the

business should be in excess of what it would earn in, say, a savings account.

Having established how much is to be invested in the business and when, the right type of finance must be selected, applied for and secured. See Chapter 8. Key projections in this area should include:

● *A cash flow forecast* – this lists all monies coming in and going out of the business, along with monthly balances. This document is an indispensable planning tool for, as we have discussed, the availability of sufficient cash resources is vital for business survival.

● *Projected balance sheet*s – the balance sheet lists for any given point in time what the business possesses (assets) and how it is financed (liabilities). Two balance sheets are required:

    – One for start-up – this will clearly show what investment is required on Day One of the business and how it will be used.

    – One for the end of the first year's trading – this will show the business's expected financial health after the first 12 months. This, along with the projected profit and loss account, should substantiate the business's financial objectives.

Business organization and control

Once objectives and plans have been set in marketing and sales, costs, profit, investment and finance, you will need to put into place systems to carry out your plans. You will need systems and policies for:

● maintaining the security of cash and merchandise
● recording all transactions in the business
● monitoring sales
● ordering goods
● selecting, training and managing staff
● handling complaints
● conforming to legislation affecting your business

Summary

The key reason for failure of small businesses is the failure to plan. The mistakes that small businesses make are testimony to this. How formal you make the planning process is largely up to you and will depend on the nature and scale of your business. However, you will be well advised to accord with the general planning principles given in this chapter. In particular, you should clearly identify the constraints on your overall business plan and develop objectives to minimize the threats posed and maximize the opportunities presented. In addition, you should now be aware of some of the major areas of concern, the importance of thinking through decisions and how a decision in one area can affect decisions taken in others. The rest of the book, which can be referred to in any order, will take you through the detailed planning you need to do.

Careful planning now will:

● minimize problems and risk
● help prevent you from making potentially ruinous moves
● raise your confidence in your ability to start up and run your business
● provide you with a framework which, when your business is up and running, will help you to identify and avoid potential problems before they happen

Finally, as indicated in the following diagram, planning is not a process that ends when you eventually open your business but one that should continue throughout its life.

Summary of the business planning process

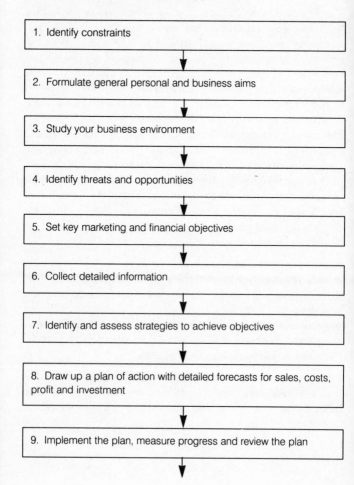

1. Identify constraints

2. Formulate general personal and business aims

3. Study your business environment

4. Identify threats and opportunities

5. Set key marketing and financial objectives

6. Collect detailed information

7. Identify and assess strategies to achieve objectives

8. Draw up a plan of action with detailed forecasts for sales, costs, profit and investment

9. Implement the plan, measure progress and review the plan

Part 2

starting your business

3

the market

What am I selling – will customers buy? • Who will buy my product? • Checklist – consumer target markets • Checklist – industrial and commercial markets • How much will they buy? • Who is the competition – what will be my market share? • When will they buy? • What price will they pay? • Summary • Checklist

In starting to investigate whether your business idea is really viable, i.e. whether it will make an acceptable profit and meet your personal requirements, you will undoubtedly be tempted to start to investigate a range of aspects at the same time, from premises, through legal requirements, to what it will cost. True, some initial groundwork should be done in all of the major areas, but little of any meaning can be achieved without some forecast of sales for your first year's trading. For instance, there is no point in looking for premises and researching costs for a large restaurant when the market will only generate trade for a smaller operation – and, of course, the question of whether the market demands a restaurant in your location is another question to be researched and answered!

To the lay person there is much mystery surrounding market research. One tends to think of it solely as the realm of the large companies and the professionals. However, nothing could be further from the truth. Market research is largely common sense; it is about finding out. Much of that finding out can be done by you, the small business person, just as well and in some cases better than by the large 'professional' market research organization. In any case, their services can run into thousands of pounds!

This chapter is designed to help you research the market for your business. Specifically, your research should help you to:

1. Refine your business idea and make sure you are offering

the right product and/or service to your market, in the right quantity, at the right price, in the right place and at the right time.

2. Forecast your sales for the start-up period and first year's trading.

To achieve these overall goals you will need to discover the answers to the following questions:

- Why will people buy my product?
- Who will buy my product?
- How much will my customers buy?
- Who is the competition?
- What are their strengths and weaknesses?
- What will my market share be?
- When will my customers buy?
- What price will my customers pay?
- Is my market growing or contracting?

What am I selling – will customers buy?

The commonest response to the first part of the question is to answer in literal terms. For instance, the owner of a small store might reply, 'What am I selling? ... that's obvious isn't it. I'm selling groceries, wines and spirits and household goods!' A response such as this is short-sighted and dangerous for a number of reasons:

- Defining your business simply in terms of the products or services it sells puts blinkers on you before you open the doors for business. It is committing the mortal sin of concentrating on what you want to sell rather than on what your customers want to buy.
- A business so blandly described lumps itself with all other businesses of a similar type. Nothing will mark it out as being different from its competitors apart from its drabness!

Therefore, to be successful, there are two simple rules:

- Define your business in terms of what your customers want to buy
- Be different from the competition

Getting the first part right is to understand the reasons why people buy. Getting the second part right is a matter of researching the competition, seeing the threats and opportunities (as we did with the wider environment in the last chapter) and building a business that concentrates on your strengths and minimizes your weaknesses.

So what do customers want? The answer is relatively simple. They buy to satisfy some need or desire. The problem, however, is more complex than most because needs are many and varied, ranging from the basic physical needs of shelter, food and safety essential for survival, through the need to satisfy personal vanity, to attainment of intellectual and spiritual satisfaction. It is said that money can't buy you love: perhaps it can't, but florists, card shops and jewellers can make a good profit helping it along the way. The cosmetics industry sells dreams of beauty, sophistication, youth – its products gratify our egos. People may buy lager to quench their thirsts, but many also buy it because it has an image that appeals and matches to a self image they aspire to. In each case the customer is motivated by the *benefits* derived from the purchase rather than the actual purchase itself. The message is **concentrate on what the product can *do* for the customer, rather than what it is.**

We have learnt that customers buy benefits and not products. However, why is it, where identical products are offered at the same price, some customers will buy from one business while others buy from another? The answer to the question is to be found in your own practical experience as a customer – try this exercise:

➤ *List as many of the factors you can that influenced your decision to buy three recent, but different, products or services. Also think about where you bought them from and finally try and isolate what influenced your choice.*

How did you get on? How many times was the decision to buy influenced solely by the benefits attached to the *product*? I would guess this affected most if not all of your choices, but not always top of the list. There will have been other reasons. Did the *price* of the purchase make a major difference or were you attracted by the convenience and availability offered by the *place* from which you bought; or was the decision more emotional than rational? Perhaps the

Fig. 3.1 To be successful you must match what you offer with what the customer wants

business's *promotion* communicated an image or life style that appealed? In the end it was no doubt a trade-off between the benefits offered by each – your mix of 'wants' matched with the marketing mix of the business from which you eventually made the purchase (as illustrated in Fig. 3.1).

This concept of the *marketing mix* provides a framework for you to build a unique selling proposition. The 'trick' is to sell the benefits that are of greatest importance to your customers. You need not meet your competition 'head on', it is unlikely that you will be able to compete in every area, rather as we have already said you should endeavour to match your strengths with the wants of a particular group of customers.

We will return to the concept of the marketing mix in the next chapter when you begin the task of putting together a marketing plan. But, before that task can begin you need to know as much as possible about your customers and the competition. However, before we leave this section it is advisable that you should make a start at defining what you are selling:

My product/service is...

I will offer..

Because my customers want...

Select one or more competitors and complete the following for each one:

Competitor's name ....

Their product/service is ....

but they also sell the following package of benefits:

Benefit	Their strength/ weakness	My strength/ weakness
Product		
Price		
Place		
Promotion		

Who will buy my product?

In the last section we saw the dangers of defining the business simply in terms of the products it sells. It is equally dangerous to describe your customers in the same terms. Defining customers solely as house buyers, drivers, smokers, machine-tool buyers, and so on is fraught with problems. Such an approach totally fails to take into account the wants of the customers concerned. Further, it lumps all users of a particular product together. Without an audit of customer wants and therefore any meaningful description of specific customer groups, businesses will attempt to compete only in the areas of price and product and ignore other aspects of the marketing mix.

We can clearly see the potentially disastrous nature of this approach when one considers what is often referred to in business circles as the 80/20 rule. The 80/20 rule or Pareto effect describes the commonly observed phenomenon that about 20% of customers account for around 80% of sales. *The task is to identify this group of people and target your efforts and resources on their wants.*

Finding the target market

Making reasoned guesses about why people may buy from

your business should have helped you focus on who those people are. For many products/services, the market can be split up into different groups of customers; that is, different *market segments*. An often-used analogy is to imagine the market as a large orange – you can peel an orange and separate it into segments. There are many ways, too, of segmenting the market.

Age

This is obvious where your product by its nature is aimed at a specific age group, for example toys, children's clothes, holidays for the retired, etc. As a general rule, people at different ages have different needs. The retired couple may have a greater need for durability and reliability while a young couple with a family and a tight budget may have low cost as a priority. Your product may appeal to different age groups for different reasons.

Sex

Will your customers be mainly women or men? Again, obvious if your product by its nature is aimed at a specific sex, for example men's or ladies' clothing. But pause for thought. The purchase of the product is not always the end-user, for instance it is well known that many women buy clothes for their husbands, sons and boy friends.

Location

Often, and in particular with any kind of retailing business, you can define your customers by where they live, work and where they go. For instance, a fast-food outlet would ideally be located near to clubs, bingo halls, places of work (to cater for meal breaks, etc.), night clubs and drinking venues; a sports shop next to a sports centre, and so on.

Occupation/employment

Research has shown that there are varying degrees of correlation between a person's occupation and tastes/attitudes. Which social class or occupational group image is your product going to appeal to?

Income

Not many businesses appeal to all ranges of income.

Obviously, if your business is going to focus on high-priced quality products your customers will more than likely be in a high-income bracket.

Leisure activities

With a growing number of people taking early retirement, becoming unemployed, working shorter hours, receiving longer holidays and enjoying better standards of living, the leisure industry is an ever-growing one. You may find it useful to define your customers according to their leisure activities, specifically as participants in certain sports or in general, for example, 'healthy-living types'.

Usage

A useful form of defining your market is by identifying segments based on the way your product is used by your customer. On a simple level, heavy use/medium use/low use/or skilled use/unskilled use. For example, a firm producing body filler for cars might find it has a number of different markets based on usage: a frequent low-skill user ('botchers'); a high-skill infrequent user (perfectionists); and a high-skill large-quantity user (trade market). Each of the three markets will have different characteristics and needs. Research might uncover that the low-skill frequent user is the largest market and is predominantly made up of non-manual working, low-income bracket owners of low-value old cars.

Checklist – consumer target markets

Make a first attempt to segment the market for your business using the process (or similar) below.

The product/service is bought:
1. frequently as an everyday essential?
2. as a treat or luxury?
3. most often as a gift?
4. only bought after long and serious consideration?
5. on the advice of others?
6. and used only by the customer?
7. often on impulse without much thought?
8. to help the customer enjoy their leisure time?

9. to help the customer enjoy a better life-style?
10. to save the customer time and make domestic chores easier and possibly fun?
11. to save the customer money?
12. to solve practical problems?
13. to deal with emergencies?
14. always for the same purposes/uses?
15. for many different purposes/uses?
16. to help the customer belong to a social group, attain a particular life-style or image?

The customers who buy this product/service can be most usefully described by:

1. sex?
2. age?
3. marital status, and number of children?
4. household site?
5. living accommodation (house, flat, mortgage, rented)?
6. neighbourhood type?
7. income?
8. disposable income (have they got spare cash or are they on a tight budget)?
9. occupation, unemployed, retired?
10. education?
11. membership of clubs and associations?
12. what they do with their leisure time?
13. what they do and where they go to socialize?
14. participation in sporting activities?
15. religious activity and beliefs?
16. ethnic group?
17. local/regional customs and traditions?
18. political beliefs?
19. environmental concerns?
20. life-style aspirations?

Industrial and commercial target markets

An often-made mistake is the belief that industrial customers are only motivated by the technical features and price of the product. Certainly, such considerations are important, but are relatively meaningless outside the context of the factors that surround the product's usage and ultimate value to the purchaser.

It is crucial to identify the relative influence of the user over the purchaser in the decision to buy. Particularly in larger companies it is often the case that the user and purchaser will operate in different spheres of the company, be constrained in different ways, and have to meet different objectives. What decisions will the buyer make when working within a purchasing budget while trying to meet usage specifications from a production engineer?

Since customers in industrial markets will be known by name, the best place to start is with a thorough analysis of each. A 'profile' should be compiled for each one. The information contained in each profile will of course vary depending on the type of market. Use the following checklist to help you profile industrial and commercial customers.

Checklist – industrial and commercial markets

Customer profile for . . . .

1. Customer's type of business (e.g. manufacturer, wholesaler, retailer, service, etc.).
2. SIC code (Standard Industrial Classification) as applicable. Note that useful information can be gained about activity in each industrial sector by reference to published statistics (see later in this chapter).
3. Number of employees.
4. Sales turnover.
5. Customer's market (N.B. the demand generated in industrial markets is ultimately derived from consumer markets).
6. Who presently supplies this potential customer?
7. Products/services normally purchased.
8. Uses to which they are put.
9. User requirements (key benefits sought – translated into key technical features as appropriate).
10. Importance to the customer of:
    - price
    - quality
    - reliability
    - support services
11. Typical order size.
12. Frequency of purchase.

13. Geographic location (quantify the cost of distribution if appropriate).
14. Other considerations?

Guidelines for selecting a target market

Whatever characteristics you use to define your target markets, they must be able to pass the following tests:

● Can the segment be measured? Will you be able to estimate the number of customers in each segment? If you have used any kind of demographic (population) characteristics in your market profile, such as age, sex, location, etc., this should be relatively easy (see p. 56. 'How much will they buy?'). Measuring a segment becomes much more difficult if it is solely defined by such a characteristic as taste in fashion.

● Is the segment of a significant size? To make the point, a target market consisting of two people, unless each represents a large potential revenue earner (i.e. a large business customer), is absurd. Nonetheless, it is possible to become over-enthusiastic and define too many target markets, resulting in confusion.

● Is the segment a potentially profitable one? There is little point in having a large target market that has little ability to purchase your product or service. The definition of market need also includes the ability to pay (see pp. 67 and 56, 'What price will they pay?' and 'How much will they buy?').

● Will you be able to gain access to the segment? It is not enough to know that the segment exists, that it is 'out there somewhere'. It is important that you can reach, communicate and sell to the identified target market. Some markets are effectively cut off from newcomers or at least very difficult to get into. For instance, many central and local government departments have to select from an approved list of suppliers.

Some large companies can provide good business but are notorious as slow payers (usually small businesses cannot afford to have their cash tied up this way). Some segments that are widely scattered geographically present too large a distribution problem (see Chapter 4, *Selling to your customers*).

Having problems?

If you have found great difficulty in defining your market and its different segments, is it because the description of your business is too vague, narrow or broad? If this is not the reason, is it because you are simply not sure what customer groups, categorized by demographic (income, age, sex, etc.), psychological (tastes, interests, etc.), geographical and usage characteristics, are seeking the benefits your product potentially offers? If it is the first of the two reasons, then go back to your business ideas and give it more thought. If it is the second, then perhaps you need to approach the problem of market segmentation from a different direction – by first identifying customer groups by specific needs in the general area of your line of business, then shaping your business idea to provide benefits to meet those needs (see Chapter 1, p. 6 *Spotting a gap in the market*).

Finding out

Even if you have made a good armchair analysis of your market segments you will no doubt want them verified. There are a number of ways of doing this. Here we will consider the use of survey techniques, primarily questionnaires and simple methods of observation, and the use of information in the form of existing surveys and statistics.

If you have made little headway in identifying your market but feel you have a good business idea, a good starting point is to observe the competition's customers in some structured way. From simple observation it is possible, depending on the type of business being researched, to deduce the customers' age, sex, time of visit, mode of transport and even the type of purchase made. From the quality and style of clothing and general image it is also possible to make some subjective stab at their income group.

Careful noting of the benefits the competition offers will also provide a useful guide to who their customers are. Your research can also be enhanced if you serve a simple questionnaire on a sample of the customers to find out more about them.

Guidelines – devising questionnaires

● *Don't* make the mistake of starting with the questions without really being clear about what you want to find out. Questions are often written down because they sound good not because they will find out what the research wants to know. Take some time first to detail exactly what you want to find out.

Have clear objectives

● *Include a means of identifying customer groups* by some tangible and measurable factors such as age, location, occupation, business activity, and so on.

● *Keep it short.* Otherwise the respondent will become bored and give inaccurate information.

● *Make it clear.* Never ask two questions in one. Always test the questionnaire on a small group to see if any questions are misleading, confusing, likely to have two meanings, suggest an answer, etc.

● *Evaluate the effectiveness of each question against objectives before use.* When the questionnaire is complete go over it again and ask of each question: *'Why am I asking this question, what useful information will it give me?'* Modify or discard any questions that don't pass this test.

● *Remember the information collected will later have to be collated and analysed.* Therefore, where it is appropriate give the respondent a range of responses to choose from. This makes it easier to sort the questionnaires after the survey.

When designing questions it is important to select the right 'type' of question to elicit the information you require. Let's consider the alternatives.

1. The yes/no question. These are closed questions offering only two responses. For example:

Do you use Carbon Filters? YES NO (please circle)

This type of question is of limited value and should be used sparingly. It is often used at the beginning of the questionnaire to 'qualify' the respondent against the sample criteria.

2. The multiple choice question. These are closed questions but offer more than two responses. For example:

How many Carbon Filters do you use each week?

> *less than 100*
> *100 to 200*
> *201 to 300*
> *301 to 400*
> *401 to 500*
> *500 +*

The structuring of the responses allows easy collating of information.

3. Scale and semantic response questions. These allow the respondent to exercise some freedom in response. They are useful for obtaining information on attitudes, opinions, motivations, perception, etc. For example:

How would you rate your present supplier of Carbon Filters on product quality?

poor . . . . .very good
(please mark with a cross the point on the scale)

Similarly, you could achieve similar ends by asking them to rate the supplier on a scale of say 1 to 5.

You can often elicit responses which reflect attitudes by using an association/projective questioning technique. For example:

What word or phrase would you associate with:

> *Sainsbury. . . . .*
> *Safeway . . . .*
> *Tesco . . . .*
> *Kwik Save . . . .*

Similarly:

Please complete the sentence:
Manufacturers who use Carbon Filters. . . . .
. . . . .

4. Open-ended questions. These allow respondents tota
freedom in the way they can answer. They are often found a'
the end of a questionnaire. For example:

*Would you like to make any additional points about Carbor
Filters?*

Although the responses may be difficult to collate anc
categorize, they may well unearth important information about
the product or market that you would remain ignorant to if the
open question was not asked.

Use the library

Much can be gained from existing market research anc
published research. Somebody may have found the answers
for you already. But where do you find them? The starting
place and perhaps the most under-used resource by smal
business people (considering it is free!) is the reference
section of your local public library. Here you will find a
wealth of information:

● Central and local government statistics – giving
information such as family expenditure on different goods
and services, and population statistics (age, income groups.
geographical distribution, etc.) (see p. 56, 'How much wil
they buy?'). Some local government offices also publish
monthly or quarterly reviews of different sectors of business
Government publications of interest include:

> *Social Trends*
> *Family Expenditure Survey*
> *General Household Surveys*
> *Economic Trends*
> *Regional Trends*
> *Annual) Monthly Digest of Statistics*

Special surveys published by the Social Survey Unit of the
Central Office of Information.

. *Note:* Guides to Government Statistics can be obtainec
from HMSO bookshops.
● Larger reference libraries carry a directory of business
associations. In this you find literally thousands of trade anc
special-interest associations, some of which may be worth

contacting to find out if they can help you. Further to this, many trade associations publish periodicals and year books that may also provide useful information. Larger reference libraries also carry trade directories. These contain much information of use to the small business. For example:

Key British Enterprises – gives basic financial information about companies.

Kompass – gives a detailed classification of the products and services offered by over 40,000 companies.

Kelly's – lists literally tens of thousands of businesses but gives little information about each company.

BRAD (British Rate and Data) – lists advertising rates and audience figures for main UK newspapers, journals, magazines, TV, radio and other media. In addition, BRAD publish a *Direct Marketing Directory* which contains extensive information on companies offering direct marketing services (e.g. mailing lists).

● The marketing, business and social science sections of the library will also be worth a scan. A search in these sections may reveal some interesting research work relating customer preferences and attitudes to your particular type of business. If you have a university or college library nearby it is not uncommon to find that members of the teaching staff or students have carried out local research in your area of business – pay it a visit, most of the hard work could have been done for you!

● Many organizations publish market reports. Two of the best known are:

MINTEL – publishes monthly market reports. Each report covers a number of consumer markets

KEY NOTE – publishes market reports on both industrial and consumer markets

Specialist publications of possible interest include:

Marketing	*Industrial Marketing Digest*
Marketing Week	*Which?*
Retail Distribution Management	

Quarterly Economic Reviews published by the main clearing banks (usually free to customers).
The Economist

The prospect of so much 'information' to search through to find what you want can be frightening, like looking for a needle in a haystack. Don't be put off; there is help at hand. Most library assistants are only too pleased to help; they are professionals and know how to track down information. If you approach them in a polite manner they will usually go to great lengths to find the information for you. However, be prepared to spend the equivalent of a full day at the library and do not be too disappointed if you do not find exactly what you are looking for.

Taking your reasoned guesses about which market segments exist, you can test your idea directly on a sample of each segment and record their reactions. This can be done by use of a questionnaire served personally, by post or telephone; or, better still, if possible, show potential customers a sample of your proposed product/service.

How much will they buy?

This is the really crucial question of how big (in revenue terms) the total market is for your business venture. The answer to the question is inextricably linked to the answer to the following questions:

- how many potential customers are there in each segment
- what quantities will they buy?
- who is the competition?
- what are my competitors' strengths and weaknesses?
- what will be my market share?

As with all marketing research there is no way you can guarantee totally reliable and accurate answers to these questions. However, the more thought you give to selecting the right methods and the more thorough your research, the more accurate your answers are likely to be.

How many potential customers are in each market segment?

The first step is to attempt to define the catchment area or location of each market segment – if you know where they are, you can count them You may have done this already in defining each target market. If not, then you must attempt to do this now.

The task of identifying where each segment is located is made easier if it includes some demographic characteristics, e.g. age, sex, housing, work place, occupation, transport, etc. With this information you can search through central and local government statistics to pinpoint concentrations of the particular characteristic you are looking for. A business selling baby clothes would look for high-population concentrations under the age of five. A property repair business would probably look for high concentrations of 'old' housing stock. Conversely, you can sometimes readily identify the prevalence of the characteristic in the area in which you trade, giving you directly the actual number of potential customers in your trading area.

➤ Are any of your market segments defined wholly or in part by any of the following?

● Age, sex, occupation, marital status, size of family or place of birth of potential customers
● People living in certain types of accommodation
● House owners
● Students
● Unemployed
● Owners of hotels
● Single parents
● Car owners
● Owners of more than one car
● People living on their own of a certain age
● Users of specific types of transport
● People living in households above a certain size
● People living in households with or without certain amenities
● Households with only one adult
● Age of a potential customer's house

If you can define your market segments by any of these characteristics by reference to the *Census County Report* (again available at your local reference library) you will be able to ascertain the number of potential customers with the required characteristics in your area. The *Census County Report* breaks this information down to local level, so the figures are available for cities, towns, and districts. The preceding list is not exhaustive and you are recommended to study your local *Report* at length. If nothing else, you will find the vast array of information on your local area interesting besides being informative.

Some care must be taken when drawing conclusions from all published statistics. With reference to census statistics, these can be anywhere between one and 10 years out of date, so for instance the 10,000 children being listed as under five years old in 1981 will be buying pop records and teenage fashion in 1991 and will have little use for baby clothes and push chairs! Mistakes like this are easy to make.

Care must also be taken in estimating the market size in relation to the proposed scale of your business. It would be unrealistic to assume that a whole city or town will represent a potential market for a small retail outlet (unless it was of a highly specialized nature with few competitors). The main catchment area in this case is probably going to be limited to a few miles radius around the proposed location. Therefore, in cases like this census statistics should be used only as a general indicator. However, as markets covering a small geographic area can be easily surveyed (very accurately) by yourself with the help of wife/husband or friend. I suggest the following simple method.

● Select a possible location for your business.

● Divide the area up into sections by drawing circles at suitable intervals, say one, two, three and four miles, or split the area into housing groups or similar (e.g. house types, prosperity). You can do both if you wish.

● Compile a questionnaire to identify who will buy, how many will buy, how much and when in each area.

● Select a random sample of say 50 in each section.

● Serve the questionnaire.

● Collate the results by totalling the responses for each section – noting the frequency of any unexpected characteristics that may suggest an alteration in your definition of the target market.

● Express all results as a percentage of the number of questionnaires served in each area. For example, convert 20 out of 80 householders within a one-mile radius who said they would purchase from your business at least once a week to 25% (20/80 100).

● Identify from your sample who will buy from your business. For example, 80% of all households sampled within a one-mile radius; 40% of all car owners interviewed; 90% of all businesses with more than 10 employees, etc.

● Carry out a physical count, or informed estimate if this is not practical, of all potential customers with these characteristics.

● Multiply the result by the percentage of positive responses from the questionnaire to obtain the actual size of the potential market for your business. To give a simple example:

(a) if from your sample 80% cf all households interviewed within one mile of your proposed site said they will buy from your business once a week; and
(b) there are 250 households within one mile of your business; then
(c) it can be estimated that you will have 200 customers from within one mile of your business per week (250 × [80/100] = 200).

Your research work can be further supported by again referring to businesses similar to your own.

Find out how much existing businesses are selling

Go to your local business estate agents and collect details on a number of businesses similar to your proposed venture. These details will usually contain sales figures for the last three years (if they don't, ask for them). Of course, accounts can be inaccurate, but if you take an average of the sales figures for a number of businesses you should be able to obtain a reasonably accurate figure for that type and size of business.

If you are planning to start a bigger business, aiming at a larger market, or your customers are going to be fairly large businesses, you can obtain valuable information from competitors' or customers' company accounts. By law, limited companies have to file copies of their accounts each year with Companies House, 55 City Road, London EC1Y 1BB. You can see or obtain by post copies of these accounts for a small fee.

Talk to people in a similar business

Try to find out what you can by meeting and talking to as many people as possible. For instance, you can view a business as a prospective purchaser and ask pertinent questions about its operation. Sometimes valuable information can be gained from people who work for, rather than own, the business – they perhaps will have less interest in guarding the business's secrets. Also, talk to members of the local trade association – you will find the number in your local telephone directory.

Review published statistics

In particular, the state-produced *Business Monitors* (available at your local reference library) cover the main business sectors. These contain a great variety of information but importantly give data such as profits, sales and costs by type and size of business. Obviously, if you can identify your category of business in one of the *Monitors* you can obtain an indication of the size of market you can expect. However, treat this as an indication only – it must be backed up by further research.

What quantities will they buy?

Having identified your target markets and the number of actual customers they will produce, you will need to establish their purchasing power. To know how many customers are in each target market is not the same as knowing how much they will buy The purchasing power of any given market is the result of the actual number of customers multiplied by their expenditure in that market in a given time period. Although you may have gone some way to establishing the purchasing power of your target markets, by virtue of the fact that many of the questions about the market for your business are interrelated, you will find the further methods introduced here will help you to determine your potential customers' expenditure on the products/services you intend to sell.

If your market consists of consumers (i.e. the general public) rather than business customers, then an excellent source of information to establish purchasing power is the state-produced *Family Expenditure Surveys (FES)* available at your central reference library. These show in great detail the income and expenditure by type of household of a comprehensive range of consumer goods and services. The information is available for the UK and includes a number of regional analyses, and is published each year.

Note of caution: When calculating approximations of market purchasing power using statistics compiled for larger areas than your envisaged market, you should always attempt to use an alternative method to verify the results. Your local area may be wholly untypical of regional and national spending patterns/trends. Does average household expenditure for your market segments as quoted in the *FES* roughly correspond to information you have derived from other market research sources/techniques? If not, why not? What are the reasons? Which is the more reliable source?

Who is the competition – what will be my market share?

Knowing the purchasing power for your market is one thing, but estimating your potential share of it is another. In practically all cases, markets are shared with competitors. You must now attempt to find out as much as you can about your competition.

In the preceding sections we have already taken a look at the competition to help shape your business and identify its markets. Hopefully, therefore, you will have already gone some way to:

1. Noting who your competitors are and where they are located.
2. Identifying how they meet their customers' needs (the benefits they provide) and how well they do it.

You will need to know as much as you accurately can about each competitor's prices, turnover, profitability, product/service range, specific details (specifications etc. of their main products/services), selling methods, and so on. Moreover, you will need to compare the strengths and weaknesses of the competition with your business. It is best if you have some structured way of doing this.

➤ *First take an overview of how well the shape of your envisaged business venture is going to match up to your potential customers' needs. This will force you to identify and profile your business's strengths and weaknesses in relation to your envisaged market. Complete the profile in Fig. 3.2 for*

Here list the features/attributes that potential customers will be looking for in your type of business/product service	Score how important each attribute is to your customers	Score your product/service on each attribute
	1 2 3 4 5	1 2 3 4 5
	1 2 3 4 5	1 2 3 4 5
	1 2 3 4 5	1 2 3 4 5
	1 2 3 4 5	1 2 3 4 5
	1 2 3 4 5	1 2 3 4 5

Fig. 3.2

your business. As a guide, the features/attributes important to your customers may include colour, taste, smell, quality, ease of use, presentation and appearance, delivery, opening times, payment terms and price. When you have scored each attribute, join up the respective ratings with a pencil line to obtain two clear profiles, one for customer preferences, one for the strengths and weaknesses of your business.

Try and be as objective and consistent as you can, avoid the temptation to pretend your business idea is other than it is.

You can of course compile a more detailed analysis by extending and modifying the profile to suit your particular business. Further, it is a good idea to compile a number of profiles, one for each of your major market segments. This will enable you clearly to see:

1. Which market segment you satisfy best.
2. Which market segment you satisfy better than the competition.

If you can identify a market segment where you are strong in both of these two areas you are likely to take a larger share of this market away from the competition than otherwise would be the case. (How you would actually go

Features	Your business	Competitor	Competitor	Competitor	Average score of competition
	1 2 3 4 5	1 2 3 4 5	1 2 3 4 5	1 2 3 4 5	1 2 3 4 5
	1 2 3 4 5	1 2 3 4 5	1 2 3 4 5	1 2 3 4 5	1 2 3 4 5
	1 2 3 4 5	1 2 3 4 5	1 2 3 4 5	1 2 3 4 5	1 2 3 4 5
	1 2 3 4 5	1 2 3 4 5	1 2 3 4 5	1 2 3 4 5	1 2 3 4 5
	1 2 3 4 5	1 2 3 4 5	1 2 3 4 5	1 2 3 4 5	1 2 3 4 5
	1 2 3 4 5	1 2 3 4 5	1 2 3 4 5	1 2 3 4 5	1 2 3 4 5
	1 2 3 4 5	1 2 3 4 5	1 2 3 4 5	1 2 3 4 5	1 2 3 4 5
Totals:					

Fig. 3.3

about capturing that larger market share is to be found in Chapter 4.)

➤ *Using similar formats (Figs. 3.3 and 3.4) to the one you have just used, analyse the threats (their strengths) and opportunities (their weaknesses) your competition presents.*

The first method shown follows the same procedure used to assess your business in relation to its market. It has the advantages of being fairly simple to compile and shows the results in a clear graphic form. Each profile is totalled to provide a single set of figures to make overall comparisons between competitors, your business and each competitor, and your business and the strength of the overall competition.

The second method's (Fig. 3.4) advantage over the first is that it takes into account the relative importance of each feature to the market. It is slightly more complicated to construct but should provide more accurate results. Use both methods and compare the results.

Method 2:

(a) Give each feature a weighting from 1 to 5 to signify its importance to the market segment.

(b) Award points, on a scale of 1 to 5, to each business, including your own, on how strong they are in each area.

(c) Multiply the importance weighting by the points awarded for each business to obtain its score.

(d) Finally, total each business's score and analyse the results.

Features	Importance	Your business		Competitor		Competitor	
		Points	Score	Points	Score	Points	Score
Totals:							

Fig. 3.4

Calculating the market share – your ability to compete with your competitors to appeal to customer-buying motives

It is possible to estimate your market share using the results of your assessment of the strengths and of the competition in satisfying the market. The principle is based on the assumption that you will capture a market share that is equal or in proportion to your ability to satisfy that market. For example, if the results of your analysis (regardless of which method is used) revealed the following total scores:

Your business:	30
Competitor 1:	10
Competitor 2:	40
Competitor 3:	30
Competitor 4:	20
Total:	130

Then it could be estimated that your business has the potential to capture 23.1% of the market based on its ability in relation to its competitors to satisfy that market – to appeal to customer-buying motives. If total market expenditure is currently £3000 per week, you will therefore expect to achieve a turnover of £693 per week. To put it another way, there is probably potential for you to gain three times the market share of competitor 1, but only three quarters of the turnover of competitor 2, and so on.

Unfortunately, there is no mathematical certainty about this method. However, it is much better than taking a stab in the dark. Its accuracy will depend on the following factors:

● How accurate you have been in identifying and ranking the need (buying motives) of your potential customers
● How accurate you have been in your assessment of your business and its competitors
● How sensitive market share is to customer preferences.

	Score	Share (%)	In £s
Your business:	30	23.1	693
Competitor 1:	10	7.7	231
Competitor 2:	40	30.7	921
Competitor 3:	30	23.1	693
Competitor 4:	20	15.4	462
Totals:	130	100.00	3000

Fig. 3.5

Calculating the market share for your business on its proportionate ability, in relation to its competitors, to satisfy customer need.
Total purchasing power of the market: £3000 per week.

➤ *To build up a clearer picture of the market, display your results in a table similar to that shown in Fig. 3.5. Compare the results to estimates of market shares obtained from some other source. Do they differ markedly? If so, why? Which do you think is the most reliable? Why? Should you err on the side of caution and take the lower of the two estimates for your business?*

Calculating your initial market share

It is unlikely that from the start-up of your business you will do better than any of your competitors. Therefore, your initial maximum market share will be no greater than:

$$\frac{\text{Total purchasing power (expenditure) of the targeted market}}{\text{Number of competitors plus 1 (your business)}}$$

In the example in Fig. 3.5 the initial weekly market share would be:

$$\frac{£3000}{5} = £600$$

In most cases, initial trading in the first few months would probably be well below this figure. Research has shown that most businesses take between six and twelve months to achieve their expected sales target. After three to six months, if your trading strategies are effective, you can expect to increase your market share in line with your ability to appeal to customer-buying motives.

When will they buy?

No matter how good your projections of what your average weekly takings or first year's sales will be, they will be of little real value if you do not know exactly when these sales will occur. Knowing what pattern of sales you will have is crucial for a number of reasons, primarily so you can plan:

- your cash requirements (see Chapter 7)
- to supply the right goods/services at the right time
- your stock levels
- your staffing requirements
- your opening times

● your sales promotion plan/campaign (see Chapter 4)

It is extremely unlikely your business will have the same sales each and every week. Both the type of products and services sold and the volume in which they are sold can vary quite considerably over different time periods. Extreme examples are toys at Christmas, fireworks around 5 November and 4 July, fresh produce according to season. Smaller time variations in demand are of no lesser importance to business planning. The generally recognized fact that most people do their shopping towards the end of the week has obvious implications for staffing levels on different days. The pattern of demand for your particular product or service can be ascertained by using a number of different sources, some of which we have already considered in previous sections in this chapter:

● General seasonal changes in demand in broad product/service groups on a national scale can be identified by using government statistics. You will easily find a table giving seasonal variation in consumer expenditure on broad product/service groups in a current copy of the *Digest of Statistics*. From the relevant *Business Monitors*, you will be able to gather more detailed information.

● If you will be purchasing stock from wholesalers or manufacturers, they will be able to supply you with detailed information on patterns of demand for their goods from their sales records and years of experience in that sector of business.

● Again trade and business associations will be able to provide information from the wealth of experience of their individual members.

● The inclusion of this goal in all your market research techniques, customer questionnaires, etc. will provide valuable information.

● Ultimately, as your business starts up and progresses, your own well-kept sales records will supply you with most of the information you need.

What price will they pay?

It is a pity that most small businesses regard competitive pricing as the main key to generating sales and profit.

However, it is only one factor among many that affects customers' buying decisions – our examination of why people buy certain products and services has revealed that much. This doesn't dispute the fact that price is a very important means of communication between your business and its potential customers; on the contrary, it is a significant part of your marketing/sales promotion strategy. Rather, it means you don't necessarily have to make your product cheap to attract customers.

Certainly low price may be the most important buying motive in relation to some products/services, but not in all cases. For instance, it is commonly known that in the case of high-quality products and services a low price can have an inverse effect on sales. A low price will force the customer to question the quality of product or service: 'Why is it so cheap?' The lesson to be learnt is that all your marketing messages should be consistent with one another, a subject we will return to in Chapter 4.

The price at which products and services sell is a prime financial consideration as well. Too low a price and you may fail to make an acceptable profit, no matter what level of sales you achieve; too high a price and you may fail to generate a viable level of sales.

So how do you decide on what price to charge? Like all aspects of planning for your business, your decision must be based on sound goals. The overall goal behind long-term pricing decisions should be to maximize profits by putting into effect pricing policies that will result in the best combination of sales volume, price and costs, while at the same time conforming to the business's overall image. How to achieve this optimum combination is partly the subject of another chapter (see Chapter 6). However, I would not wish this to mask the importance of the subtle use of price to achieve a number of short-term goals:

● To increase sales volume. Typically, short-term price reductions to help build the business – obviously there will be a cost element to this.
● To obtain differential pricing/profit maximization. Often different pricing policies can be adopted for different target markets. Two of the many well-known examples are cheap tickets on off-peak period travel and different telephone

tariffs for business and commercial users. There is potential for implementing different pricing structures/policies where target markets are sufficiently dissimilar and either sympathetic to such a policy, as in the case of price reductions for senior citizens, or unaware of the policy, as in the case where target markets are geographically widely dispersed. At all costs, where such a policy is implemented, profitable customer groups should not be antagonized.

● To maximize unit profit. This is where target markets are selected mainly on the basis of their willingness to pay high prices. Physical volume is sacrificed to obtain a high unit profit on each sale.

● To protect the business from new competitors entering the market. The business may adopt a short-term pricing policy which reduces profits but makes it difficult for a new company threatening to come into the market to gain a foothold.

Many new businesses will take the lead from their competitors, letting them set the price. The main golden rule not to break when starting up is not to set your prices too low. You can always reduce prices but to raise them is more difficult!

Summary

The importance of establishing a complete profile of your potential market cannot be overstated. Without such detailed information, it is meaningless to attempt to cost the project and establish profitability. Also the size and nature of the market will dictate the resources your business needs and therefore the nature and size of the overall investment.

Identifying the characteristics of your target markets, including their potential size, is one thing; converting them into actual sales is another. It is to this task that we turn our attention in the next chapter, where you will use the information gained from your research to put together a detailed marketing plan for your business.

Checklist

The plan

1. What are your marketing research objectives?
2. What techniques/methods are you going to use to research the information?
3. Are they valid (will they find out what you want)?
4. Are they reliable?
5. How will you attempt to verify the results?
6. How will you use the results to modify your business idea?

The questions

1. Why will people or businesses buy your product?
2. Who are your potential customers?
3. Who is the end-user?
4. Who makes the decision to buy?
5. Where are your potential customers?
6. How much will they buy?
7. How often will they buy?
8. What will they use the product or service for?
9. What are their major needs?
10. Do they control their buying behaviour?
11. How many different customer groups (market segments) can you identify?
12. What is the size of each market segment in revenue terms?
13. Per year, per month, per week, per,.,.,.,?
14. What will be your market share?
15. How important is price to each market segment?
16. What package of benefits will each segment be looking for?
17. Is the market growing or contracting?
18. What method of distribution (selling method) does the market suggest?
19. What business image does the market most favourably react to?
20. How much will you earn from sales and when in your first year's trading?

The techniques available

1. Questionnaire – what will be its objectives?
2. How will it be implemented (telephone, door-to-door, etc.)?

3. What are the characteristics of the sample interviewed?
4. Have you made sure that the sample has the same characteristics as your envisaged target market?
5. How will you make sense of the information collected?
6. Will you use some method of observation (e.g. customer count, etc.)?
7. Have you identified the competition?
8. What have you learned from detailed observation of the competition?
9. Have you collected trading figures for similar businesses that are for sale in the area?
10. Have you checked out the usefulness of the statistics on population and consumer expenditure?
11. Have you spoken to any local business people?
12. Have you checked and read any trade publications in your area of business?

4

selling to your customers

A framework for a marketing plan – the marketing mix

The methods presented in Chapter 3 should have helped you identify viable market segments in some detail. You will now need a practical plan to enable you to capture a worthwhile share of those markets. We can start to build the framework for such a plan by asking four basic questions.

To get potential customers to buy my product or service in sufficient numbers:

1. What benefits will my product or service have to offer potential customers?
2. What price is the product or service going to be offered at and how important is price in influencing potential customers' buying motives?
3. How is the product or service going to be sold? From what place or by what means?
4. How is the launch of my business going to be promoted/publicized to its market segments?

Satisfactory answers to these questions will provide a recipe for ensuring potential customers are turned into actual customers. The recipe is a well-known one, and is often referred to as the marketing mix or the four Ps:

Product: The benefits the product offers must fulfil the needs of your customers – otherwise why should they buy your product or service?

Price: Your customers may need your product or service, but can they afford it?

Place: Your product must be sold in a location that is both accessible and attractive to your customers. Such a place, depending on the nature of your market, may range from a shop in the city centre to individual customers' homes. The way the product is sold is also an important consideration.

Promotion: There is little point in getting the product, price and place right if your customers don't know you exist. The right advertising is certainly important but is not the only factor in sales promotion as we will see later.

Let's consider each factor or variable in the marketing mix in more detail.

Product and service decisions

Whatever you are selling, whether it be groceries, a haircut, general domestic repairs, washing machines or even something as seemingly simple as bricks, getting the product or service right is a matter of thinking about what it does rather than what it is.

➤ *What are the features of your business, product or service?*

➤ *What will they do for a potential customer?*

➤ *Will the customer need what you are offering?*

Listing the features of your product or service provides a detailed breakdown of what it is. For instance, the features of a microwave oven might include 'a pre-programmable timer' and 'available in a range of colours'. Identifying what these features can do for the customer itemizes the benefits of buying and using such a product. For the microwave, the following might be true:

Features	*Benefits*
Pre-programmable timer	Will cook your meal for you even when you are not at home
Available in a range of colours	Can be matched to any kitchen colour scheme

73

Whether or not the customers will buy depends partly on whether what is being offered is what they want. If the following is true, then the microwave has a good chance of selling:

Features	*Benefits*	*Needs of the market segment*
Pre-programmable timer	Will cook your meal for you even when you are not at home	Working, lead busy lives – have little time to prepare and cook meals
Available in a range of 'modern' colours	Can be matched to most kitchen colour schemes	High-income 'sophisticated' group. Place importance on appearance – need to keep up with trends. Likely to have spent a lot of time and money selecting kitchen layout and colours

Identifying product benefits

- List the features of each of your products
- Identify for each feature what it may do for, or mean to the customer
- Every time you think of a feature of a product or some aspect of your business, practise using the phrase – *which means that* ... To give some examples:

The casing is made from carbon fibre *which means that* ... less time will be spent on maintenance

... ten more units can be carried per truck load *which means that* transportation costs are substantially reduced

... longer equipment life, *which means that* the product has higher re-sale value and reduced depreciation costs

The car runs on lead-free petrol and has a catalytic converter *which means that*
... the car will run on cheaper petrol
... less damage will be done to the environment
... the car meets import regulations

As you can see, any one single feature may offer several benefits. It is important to list them all, for just as a need may be satisfied in many different ways a product may be bought for many different reasons.

Without a thorough features-benefits analysis of your products and/or services it is foolhardy to attempt to make plans in other aspects of the marketing mix. This is firstly because the major determinant of the price a customer will pay is their perception of the product in terms of 'value for money'. It should be obvious that the more benefits a product or service provides that the customer wants, then the greater its 'value for money' factor will be at a given price. Secondly, a selling message, whether it be in an advertisement or part of a personal selling pitch, depends on isolating what the customer will want to buy.

Your work with the previous chapter should have provided you with ample information to complete a detailed features-benefits and customers' needs card for each main product or service you sell (see Fig. 4.1).

➤ *Armed with this information and detailed knowledge of the features of the product/service you are intending to sell, you can use the chart shown in Fig. 4.1 to see if you have got it right.*

Features	Benefits	Customers needs
What it is	What it will do	Is that what the customer needs?

Fig. 4.1 Features – benefits and cistomers' needs analysis chart

Deciding on the type and level of customer service

As the customer's decision to purchase often hinges on the services offered with the product it is essential that you should know:

● the type and level of customer service that is required by customers
● how your intended provision compares to that offered by the competition
● the cost of the proposed level of provision

Service competition offer	Importance to the customer	Cost estimate	Level of service planned
Free trials			
Samples			
Demonstrations			
Brochures/sales literature			
Design service/ pre-sale advice consultancy			
Estimates and quotations			
Customer entertainment			
Credit facilities			
Personal service			
Location/place services – customer care facilities provided			
Stock availability			
Stock range			
Trade-in options			
Delivery (time) (quantity) (frequency)			
Sale or retur options			
Discounts			
Technical support			
Spares and replacement stock			
Warranty/ guarantees			

Service competition offer	Importance to the customer	Cost estimate	Level of service planned
On-site service			
After-sales calls			
Training/ guidance in product use			
Product us information			
Complaints handling service			

Pricing decisions

Chapters 3 and 6 deal at length with the subject of price. What needs to be stated here is that it is often a falsehood to consider price as the single most important customer buying motive. You would be well advised to re-read 'What price will they pay?' (Chapter 3) and then complete the following checklist activities.

---

1. For your main products/services, find out and list the current prices being charged by your leading competitors.

Product/service	Your price	Competitor: A B C D E F
1.		
2.		
3.		
4.		
5.		

You may find that the price difference between competitors may vary from one product to another. What is the 'difference' when all the major products are considered together?

2. Is there an accepted 'market price' that the majority of the competition adheres to?

3. How sensitive do you expect your sales volume to be to changes in price?

4. What pricing policy are you going to adopt?

    (a) Accept the market price, because:
- your costs will not allow you to charge a lower price?
- you can't afford a price war?
- other?

    (b) Charge a higher price than the competition, achieve a higher gross profit on each sale while accepting a lower sales volume, because:
- you are in the rare and fortunate position that demand for the product outstrips supply?
- price is not a significant factor in affecting your customers' decision to buy?
- other factors such as quality, personal service, reliability are paramount and overriding factors affecting your customers' decision to buy?
- you have limited production/selling capacity/space available and are faced with a healthy demand for your product?

    (c) Charge a lower price than the competition, risk a 'price war', hope that a lower gross profit on each sale will be offset by increased sales, because:
- low prices are singly important to your customers?
- your unit gross profit at market prices is high so you can afford a – price war. You have low overheads and your competition doesn't?
- it is the only way you will make inroads into the market?
- you have sufficient capital resources to overcome the possible cash problems that can ensue from such action?

    (d) Charge different prices to different market segments, because:
- your target markets are sufficiently dissimilar?
- your target markets are separated by time or space?
- your target markets are sympathetic to such a move?
- your product or service is such that it can be offered in different ways and forms to different market segments?

Place and distribution decisions

This is the question of not just where but how (including at what time of the day, week or year) the product will be offered for sale. The place and the method chosen to sell a product or service, along with the product/service itself, add up to a total package of benefits offered to the customer. Most people, for example, are aware that the continued success of the small convenience store is based on benefits to the customer of place and time rather than on the individual benefits of each product it sells. The bread, milk, headache pills and toilet rolls you buy from your local convenience store at 9.30 pm on a Sunday night might be exactly the same products you can buy at a lower price from the supermarket the next morning, but when the total package of benefits, including those to the customer stemming from such facts as opening times and accessibility, are considered along with the actual product or service, it can easily be seen that the two businesses, in catering for different markets, are not 'selling' the same 'product'.

In Chapter 5, we will examine the importance of, and factors affecting, your choice of location, and from the first pages of this book I have stressed the importance of knowing what you are selling. The application of the market research techniques in Chapter 3 is important, specifically:

● 'When will they buy?' – will tell you when you should open and when you should stock and promote certain products/services.
● 'Why will they buy?' – will identify the package of benefits your market segments will be seeking.
● 'Who will buy my product/service?' – will help you decide on a suitable location.

Now we must consider the range of methods for getting your product to the customer.

Methods of distribution

Businesses use a range of different means to get their product/service to the customer. Obviously, it is important that you choose a means of distribution that is right for your market while at the same time being aware of alternatives that might gain you access to further markets.

Starting your business

Andrea and Sarah planned to go into business selling fashionable children's clothes. As a result of Sarah's experience as a buyer for a large retail group, they had identified good suppliers and were looking for a suitable method of distribution. Their first thoughts were to buy a small lock-up shop but this soon became a non-starter when they considered the limited finance available to them. So they were forced to look at the alternatives. Andrea was on a 'starting your own business' course at the local college and had a list of the major channels of distribution. They both sat down to study it with the hope of coming up with the answer for their particular business.

Retail outlet

This general term covers everything from the marketstall to large department stores and hypermarkets. The main advantages and disadvantages of selling through your own retail outlet can be summarized as follows.

Advantages

● Enables your business to be easily identified by your customers.
● Can be chosen to be in proximity to concentrations of your customers.
● Can draw on passing trade.
● The business can be more easily controlled and promoted.

Disadvantages

● Can result in high capital costs.
● It is not flexible to some changes that may take place in the market. For example, the neighbourhood can go into decline, parking restrictions might be imposed, your market can 'move away', etc.

Wholesale outlets

These perform the function of holding a large volume of stocks mainly for small retailers. The advantage to the retailer of dealing with a wholesaler rather than the manufacturer is that large chunks of working capital do not have to be tied up in stocks. Conversely, the manufacturers prefer to deal with wholesalers instead of small retailers because they are in a position to make bulk purchases. This reduces administration and physical distribution problems and thus costs for the manufacturer.

As a new small business it is unlikely that you will be able to convince a wholesaler to buy in large quantities of your untried product. However, the chief advantage of dealing with a wholesaler is that the costs involved in marketing the product direct to the consumer are taken over by the wholesaler. Obviously, your profit margin will be reduced but this should be offset by the increase in sales volume and decrease in overheads of using this method.

The main problem with this form of distribution is that you can lose control over the way the product is marketed to the final purchaser. As the level of demand set by the end purchaser will ultimately affect your sales, bad distribution by the wholesaler and poor selling practices by the retailers he sells to can have disastrous effects on your business. The same is, of course, partly true if you intend to set up as a wholesaler yourself.

You can, of course, bypass the wholesaler and sell direct to retailers. You will encounter some of the problems associated with selling to wholesalers but have the advantage of vetting each retailer in turn. To encourage retailers to give selling space to your product, you might consider offering:

● sale or return terms
● in-store merchandising – a service where you will go into their shops, help the retailer make the order, stock his fixture and in addition possibly supply display stands and promotional material. This makes you a more attractive proposition to the retailer while, at the same time, allowing you to retain some control over the way the product is marketed to the final purchaser.

Mail order

This is an increasingly popular method of distribution. It involves direct selling to customers via such mediums as TV, radio and press advertising. In most cases, the customer is encouraged to place an order using an order form attached to the advertisement.

The attraction of this method for the new small business is in the fact that costly premises don't have to be acquired.

However, the real advantages of this method is that it can be used to:

● reach and distribute to a market that is geographically scattered

● reach a wide range of market segments by choosing different advertising mediums and approaches

● allow the business to engage in differential pricing policies between market segments

● adapt quickly to changes in the market.

Further, a small business using this method does not necessarily have to buy in large quantities of stock in advance of sales. In many cases stock need only be purchased when orders and payment are received. This has the obvious advantage of greatly reducing working as well as fixed capital requirements (see Chapter 7).

There are certain disadvantages with this method; chiefly:

● advertising and sales promotion costs will be relatively high when compared to other methods

● many less than honest traders have used this method and given it bad publicity

● many products/services do not lend themselves to this impersonal method of selling.

Door-to-door selling

This is the method of distribution that everybody makes jokes about! Its popularity is on the decline, but it can and should still be considered as a possibility. The main problem is getting over the consumer's basic distrust of this method and the time involved in making each sale.

Party plan selling

This is another low-cost method of distribution that has gained popularity, particularly in the USA. Usually a company will engage agents who will organize 'parties' in their own homes, demonstrating and selling the company's products to their friends and relatives. The agent is usually paid on a commission basis and encourages customers to become agents themselves. This method can work well if carefully organized. However, the problem is its own popularity: the market place is becoming overrun with 'party plans'. For the small business, 'party plan' offers similar advantages to mail order.

After studying the various methods of distribution open to them, and much discussion, Andrea and Sarah decided to market the children's clothes initially through 'party plan'. Their reasons were as follows:

● *The needs of the market:* the purchasers of their product would be young mothers who may not be able to 'get out of the house'. They may also appreciate the opportunity to socialize with other young women in the same situation as themselves. So party plan seemed the method that might appeal to the market the most.

● *Capital considerations:* using party plan, only a range of samples needed to be purchased. Stock would only be acquired as orders were placed (remember, Sarah had identified suppliers who could be relied on). Also there was no need to raise capital for premises.

● *Financial considerations:* although transport costs would be high in making frequent visits to wholesalers, overheads should be low. As agents will be paid on a commission only basis, labour costs will vary in proportion with sales.

Keeping an eye on the future, Andrea and Sarah decided that when they had built a sound base from 'party plan' sales they would venture into mail order. The plan was to build up enough capital from these two methods to open a small retail outlet.

Did they make the right decision? Well, 18 months on Andrea and Sarah have 12 party plan agents and steady sales from that aspect of the business. Their venture into mail order was something of a disaster, finding that the promotional costs far outweighed the profits from the volume of business they brought in. They still haven't got enough capital for the shop but have managed to start a relatively successful marketstall.

➤ *What methods of distribution are you going to use to help sell your product/service? Use the following checklist to help you come to a decision.*

1. Will it meet the needs of your market segments?
2. Will it be compatible/complementary with/to other elements of your marketing mix?
3. Will it produce sufficient sales?
4. What are the working and fixed capital requirements of such a method?
5. What costs will it involve?
6. Will the method allow you to charge a price that will give you a sufficient profit margin?
7. What methods do your competitors use? Are these the right ones?
8. Will the method preclude you from controlling the way the product or service is marketed to the end purchaser? How important is this to your business?

Promotion and advertising plans

The final part of your marketing plan is the promotion of the product/service package. The first objective of any business start-up promotion plan is to tell potential customers of its existence. The second is to get them to visit it. The third is to get them to buy. The fourth is to get them to come back. This section will therefore deal with the method and means of doing this. Your overall objective is to turn the people who make up your potential target markets into loyal customers.

Developing a sales promotion plan

There are a number of key aspects to developing a sales promotion plan:

1. What do you want to happen (specifically)?
2. What message will make it happen (what message will be sent, how can it be made persuasive)?
3. What media will be used to communicate the message?
4. What will it cost?
5. What profits will it generate?
6. How can you find out if the sales promotion worked?

If you have done a good job in answering the questions posed in Chapter 3 and this chapter you should be in a fairly good position to summarize the information by answering the following two broad questions:

1. *What image will your business attempt to project?* This should be built on and from the package of benefits you are offering to your customers.
2. *By what means can potential customers be attracted away from the competitors?* By this stage you should have carried out a detailed analysis of the competition, as suggested in this chapter and in more detail in Chapter 3.

This summary will provide you with the message you wish to send to your potential customers.

What do you want to happen?

What do you want your potential customers to do?

Deciding on the message you wish to send to your customers is not as easy as it first appears. First, you must decide what you want them to do and, second, what will have to be in the message to persuade them to do what you want.

What you want them to do is really your set of specific objective(s) for the sales promotion. To help you promote your business start-up, in response to the message you send, do you want your customers to:

● note you exist?
● visit your premises?
● make requests for further information?
● make an order?
● other?

How are you going to make it happen?

Next, how are you going to persuade your potential customers to respond in a positive manner to the message? As we have stressed throughout, for products and services to sell they have to have genuine benefits for potential customers. Therefore, your best chance of getting potential customers to do what you want is to point out the benefits of becoming one of your customers. To do this you need to stress more than just the benefits of the actual product or service being offered for sale. The customer services offered by the business must also be stressed, as in the earlier example of the convenience store: the actual product did not contain the key selling points, it was the opening times and accessibility of the store to its customers that were the appealing benefits.

This persuasive message, once identified, should become the basis for building an image, something you become known for, such as:

- friendly personal service
- speed and reliability of delivery
- excellent after-sales service and backup.

This should be promoted at all times. Good advertisements and sales promotions should follow what has now become commonly known as the *AIDA* formula. For an advertisement to have a chance of success it must attract customers' *A*ttention, gain their *I*nterest which, in turn through the message being communicated, generates *D*esire to take the *A*ction of going out and buying the product.

Attention – most prospective customers scan over poor advertisements without paying attention. You need to stop this browsing with something that will focus their minds. Clever use of graphics, colours or bold headlines can sometimes achieve this.

Interest – the next step is to gain their attention long enough to transmit the central message. Concentrate on trying to relate to what your research has identified as your customers' most important needs. Try to do it in a simple but interesting way. Don't make the mistake of making the advertisement confusing and boring by trying to communicate too much – keep to the most powerful messages.

Desire – if you have managed to capture their attention long enough and the message is powerful enough, then the potential customer should feel the need to purchase the product.

Action – finally the advertisement should include some aspect that will encourage the customer to come to you and make the purchase. Many advertisements seek to do this by using such phrases as: limited offer, while stocks last, free trial, and so on. Others offer money-off coupons, or make

suggestions such as 'come down next week on our late
opening night' (including simple directions of how to get
there), or encourage the potential customer to give them a
telephone call straight after seeing or hearing the
advertisement. In fact any ploy can and should be used (as
long as it is legal and honest) to instil action in the customer.

Checklist – do-it-yourself advertising copy

1. Be clear about the objectives for the 'copy'.

2. Define the target audience.

3. Identify the most persuasive appeal. Will it be:
   - rational?
   - emotional?
   - fear?

4. Identify the most persuasive style. Will it be:
   - product in use?
   - show how product will relate to and enhance life-style?
   - enact customer fantasy?
   - reflect customer mood?
   - scientific/technical knowledge?
   - testimonial?

5. Headline. This is your chance to get the reader's attention.
   It should:
   - be very clear and state the unique selling proposition
   - lead the reader to identify with the message
   - be in the style of language the reader uses
   - match the content of the rest of the advertisement

6. Visual images used should:
   - reinforce the headline
   - visualize the theme and the message
   - have a main focal point

7. Overall, does the copy:
   - grab attention?
   - relate positively to customer beliefs and motivations?
   - identify a customer problem and offer a solution?
   - generate interest through appeal?
   - reassure that needs will be satisfied?
   - promote action – inform the customer about availability?

The media

There are many means of communicating the message to your market segments, and the choice of media is as crucial as the message itself. Each medium of communication, from personal recommendation to television, has specific advantages and limitations. Let's briefly consider some of the media available to a small business. As a rough rule of thumb, the more personal the advertising medium is, the more persuasive it is likely to be.

Personal recommendation by present customers to potential customers is perhaps the most persuasive means to attract new custom. Obviously it is not one that can be used in the start-up period but because of its power and nil cost it should be fostered with care as the business grows.

Direct 'personalized' calling by telephone or letter has the advantage of being able to target your communication precisely. It may have the effect of making a potential customer feel important and therefore more likely to respond in a positive manner. Others, however, may feel it an affront to their privacy. What would be the reaction of your target markets? Also, if the telephone is used you have the opportunity to gain direct responses to your 'message'. Your approach, of course, must be carefully constructed and practised before use.

The average response rate from direct marketing is around 2 per cent. To improve on this figure, refer to the guidelines below:

Do-it-yourself direct marketing

1. Clear market profiling is the key (see Chapter 3). Once profiles are compiled, communication media can be examined for match. If mailing lists are the preferred option then these can be compiled in many ways:
   ● from publicly available records such as the *Yellow Pages* and commercial telephone directories
   ● by contacting relevant associations and clubs whose members match your target profile (refer to association directories in your Central Reference Library). Many associations and clubs, on application and payment of a fee, will provide a membership listing

● mailing lists to fit a wide variety of audience profiles are available from a range of mail list brokers. A look through any issue of the magazine *Marketing* will reveal a number of companies advertising for business. Mailing lists are also available from large organizations such as British Telecom.

2. If buying in a mail list check:
   ● what detail the listing gives – will it allow you to send the communication you want?
   ● how up to date is the listing?
   ● what was the original purpose of the list?
   ● will you be able to sample the list?

   Communications are expensive! You don't want to find out the list mismatches after you have spent a couple of thousand pounds on a direct mail out!
   ● what track record has the listing? What reliable evidence can be produced by the broker? What has been the success rate of previous mailings?

3. Message content and presentation must be of high quality otherwise your communication will be seen as just another item of junk mail. All the guidelines that apply to message construction and presentation earlier in the chapter apply. However, remember:
   ● the singular aim of direct marketing is to get the required response
   ● the initial attention span of the recipient is likely to be low. Don't bore them to death Attention must be gained quickly and interest aroused if the rest of the communication is not to be skipped over and consigned to the waste paper bin
   ● lead with the appeal: the benefits to the purchaser or user. Don't become bogged down in aimless preamble
   ● always think what impact the whole package will have on the recipient when it is first opened
   ● keep next month's direct mail – review each piece with the aim of establishing:
   (a) examples of good practice
   (b) styles to be avoided
   ● make sure the offer is clear and unambiguous
   ● make it easy for the audience to respond by including either a return envelope or link line telephone number. Contact British Telecom for information on the 0800 service.

4. Every response must be recorded. Ideally you will need a computerized database system capable of producing personalized letters from customer records. If you know little about computers, don't pay for expensive private training courses, sometimes costing in excess of £100 per day. Enquire at your local Further Education College. A small business micro, high-quality printer and database software can be obtained for less than £3000.

The *Yellow Pages* should be an obvious medium to use, particularly for specialist small businesses. Many consumers use this as a starting point for finding goods and services. If you decide to pay for an entry it is probably worthwhile to go for a distinctive box advertisement. Consumers are more likely to investigate the obvious rather than wade through the small print. Also, it is sensible if you can justify an entry under 'A' so that it is read first instead of last

Newspaper advertising is very useful to a new business to build up awareness that it exists. The charge per advertisement can be quite high but when compared to the potential number of readers it might be that the cost per customer reached can be low. However, the problem with newspapers, and the same is true of radio and TV, is that only a small percentage of the readership may be from the target market you are aiming at. If a large part of the local population is your target market, then this is certainly a good method to use. Remember to place advertisements where your potential customers will see them – the TV page, for instance, could be a good place to advertise VTR tapes.

A mention or feature in the local newspaper can sometimes be secured by new small businesses free of charge as a 'human interest' story. This is always worth investigating.

Magazines can be a useful medium to use where the readership corresponds to your target markets. Go to your local reference library and ask if they have a publication that details the characteristics of the readership of various magazines and find out if any match up with the profiles of your target markets. One advantage of using magazines over newspapers is that the magazine will be kept for quite a long period whereas the newspaper will be discarded after a day.

The advertisement is therefore likely to be seen and read a greater number of times by each individual reader.

Local radio stations offer widespread coverage for a reasonable cost per thousand listeners. However, for effect, the advertisement would have to be repeated regularly over a period, considerably pushing up costs. If this medium is used, careful attention must be given to placing the advertisement at times when your target market is most likely to be listening.

Television is perhaps the most expensive form of advertising. However, short-duration 'spot' commercials are becoming reasonably priced. In the UK, Channel 4 provides considerable help for the first-time user.

Billboard posters are a relatively cheap form of communication. Usually you will have to pay a fee for the poster itself and then three months' rent of the billboard. If you decide to use this method, then the location must be chosen with care. Perhaps there is a large billboard close to where you plan to open your business, outside an office block where a large proportion of your target market works or on the bus route they use. Check out the site carefully: is it visible from more than just one direction, is there anything that will distract from whatever message it is attempting to send and will people have ample opportunity/time to see it? The disadvantages of using posters are:

● research has been unable to gauge their effect (the general consensus is they are not very persuasive)
● people tend to regard them as part of the background, consequently the poster itself would have to be very creative to catch a person's attention.

Leaflets have the advantage over posters of being able to be targeted at specific groups of potential customers. They are relatively cheap to produce and circulate but are often ignored by the receivers – what did you do with the last lot of leaflets that were put through your letter box? However, if you deliver to small areas at a time, it is relatively easy to monitor the results. Use the 'do-it-yourself direct marketing' guidelines to improve the effectiveness of leaflet design and distribution.

There are but a few of the main methods of communication. Here are some others for your consideration:

- Diaries
- Taxis
- Exhibitions
- Local charity magazines
- Exterior of your business vehicles
- Newsagents' windows
- Beer mats
- Milk bottles
- Litter bins
- Carrier bags
- Interior and exterior of buses
- Calendars
- Sports team sponsorship
- Packaging

►*What others can you think of? The choice is certainly vast. Any single medium used on its own will be unlikely to be sufficient. Which do you select? To help you come to a decision, use the following checklist.*

1. Is it consistent with the image of your product?
2. Will it be seen or heard in sufficient numbers by your target group?
3. What opportunities will each target group have of seeing or hearing the advertisement?
4. How many times will the target group see or hear the advertisement?
5. What is the cost of reaching each individual customer?
6. How persuasive do you consider the medium to be?
7. Can it be targeted accurately on the group you wish to use?
8. Is it complementary to other media you plan to use?

How can the success of a sales promotion/advertisement be measured?

You should monitor the outcomes of your advertising and other sales promotion activities for two reasons:

1. To compare the sales the campaign has generated against the costs involved to see whether it has been a profitable activity.
2. To see whether the sales promotion has achieved its stated goals. Then you can build on a good practice and make sure you don't make the same mistake twice.

Sales promotion plan

Objectives:

Duration (dates):

Theme or message:

Media to be used:

Cost:

In store promotional support
(or personal contract support):

Implications for business organization (e.g. capital and stock
requirements):

Method to monitor and check results:

Measuring the success

Promotion:

Duration:

Theme/objective:

Media used:

                                                                Comments
                        Total cost of campaign:
            Estimated number exposed to campaign:
Of which estimated target marketing audience:
                                Sales objective:
                            Actual sales increase:
            Variance (objective – results):

Increase in gross profits after cost of campaign (i.e. actual sales
increase x unit gross profit – total cost of campaign = £

Fig. 4.2

There are a number of ways of doing this but as a general guide you should plan and monitor your sales promotions campaigns as suggested in the tables shown in Fig. 4.2.

Media audience profiles

Information on various media audience profiles is extensively researched and made available by a number of agencies:

● The Broadcasters' Advertising Research Board (BARB) provides information on Television and Radio.

● British Rate and Data (BRAD) lists virtually all types of advertising and their costs.

● The National Readership Survey (NRS) gives information on each publication's circulation and readership.

● Target Group Index, published by the British Market Research Bureau, available on a subscription basis, gives information which relates media to buying behaviour in specific markets.

Making the sale

The simple truth that nothing happens in business unless somebody makes a sale, emphasizes the essential nature of the selling activity in the marketing mix.

Contrary to popular belief, selling skills can be learnt. It is certainly worth checking what courses are available in your locality. The alternative is to teach yourself. To this end, the following sections provide guidelines on the basic techniques of personal selling. I recommend that you study these and try to apply the techniques to your business, products and customers. As with any skill, practice will result in the development and sharpening of your personal selling technique. You will obtain the best results by role-playing sales situations (perhaps with your husband, wife, friend or colleague). You can learn a lot by doing this, particularly if you spend some time after each role-play trying to identify where you went wrong and what you did right. If you have the use of a video camera a great deal can be learnt from taping and replaying each practice session.

A goods sales person is one who understands that the terms buying and selling describe different facets of the same business transaction, where the seller solves the buyer's problem and vice-versa. Good selling practice focuses on and develops from identification of the buyer's problem. If you have successfully built the 'marketing approach' into your business operations you should have the solutions to the customer's problem, and hence the sale, within your grasp. The rest is a matter of technique!

A framework for selling

Although there are no guaranteed success formulas it is generally recognized any sale moves through several logical steps as illustrated in Fig. 4.3.

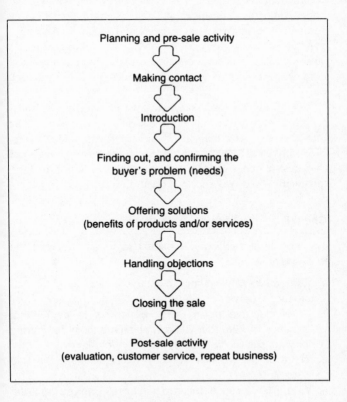

Planning and pre-sale activity

Making contact

Introduction

Finding out, and confirming the
buyer's problem (needs)

Offering solutions
(benefits of products and/or services)

Handling objections

Closing the sale

Post-sale activity
(evaluation, customer service, repeat business)

Fig. 4.3 The structure of a sale

Pre-sale activity

The starting point must be with identification of the target market (see Chapter 3). However, in the case of industrial and commercial selling it is not enough to know which organizations to target. You need to select the right person in the organization to present to. Generally your aim is to get at the decision maker – the person with the Money, Authority and Need to buy (giving the rather sexist but widely used acronym MAN).

The next requirement is that you find out as much as you can about your customer's needs. You cannot offer the solution if you don't know the problem. With industrial and commercial customers you will need to know and understand their business as well as they do. Reading company reports, trade magazines and journals, making a positive attempt to understand the threats and opportunities your prospective client faces, and knowing your competition are all part of the professional sales person's research objectives.

Out of financial necessity you must be selective. Personal selling is expensive; you must endeavour to make it cost effective by selecting the best prospects. 'Qualifying' prospective customers is a matter of short listing the ones that best match your capability to offer a solution to their 'problem' – in a way that will result in a profit to you.

Checklist – qualifying a prospect

The key to evaluating a prospect is to ask yourself the following questions:

1. Can you identify whether they have a clear need for your product or service?
2. Have they the money and willingness to pay? What evidence is there that you can persuade them that paying for your 'solution' will represent 'value for money'?
3. Will they buy in large enough volume to make the sale viable?
4. Who will make the decision to purchase? Can you get to the one person who is the MAN? Or is the problem more complex?

Getting appointments

Getting appointments is no easy matter. By far the best medium to use is the telephone. All calls should be kept short and stick to a well-rehearsed routine. The aim is to assess as many prospects as possible within a given period of time. Often a prospect will claim they are too busy to see you. The easiest way around this is to always offer an alternative time and date and then try to close the call that way. Never, ever try to overcome stronger objections; you are wasting time and money, move onto the next call. Follow a simple framework of: .

● courteous greeting and identification of company
● move quickly on to relating a single benefit to the prospect's needs
● try and close the call by offering alternative appointment date
● confirm the appointment details

The whole call should not take more than a couple of minutes.

The sales interview

First, there are some basic rules to learn and remember:

● Above all be professional in both dress and manner. Be there on time and stick to whatever promises you made when arranging the interview. If you said you would only take 30 minutes of their time don't take more.
● Don't waste time by talking about the weather or the decor of your prospect's office. Initial pleasantries are in order but should be brief. Remember when you walk into the room you have an objective to meet, you have the initiative, it is up to you to direct the interview. *Don't lose the initiative in the first few minutes.*
● Have a structure for your presentation but on the other hand don't stick religiously to some prepared script – otherwise you will come across as too smooth and slick and unbelievable – it will all appear as just so much 'salesman's talk'. Also avoid well-worn cliches such as 'this is the best product on the market ... we have hundreds of satisfied customers'.

The structure of the interview can be built around the AIDA

You	The prospect
Lead with an initial benefit statement or open question	Attention – listens and responds.
Ask 'open' questions – find out needs. Listen Ask closed questions – confirm needs.	Interest provides carefully. information
Present the solution. State your product features and benefits – show how they will solve the problem.	Desire – but may present objections.
Resolve objections and attempt to close.	Action – order placed.

Fig. 4.4 The sales interview

approach we used to effect when discussing advertising and sales promotion. The first task is to get their Attention, the second is to hold it by generating Interest, the third to develop a Desire to buy, so that you finally get the prospect to take the Action of committing themselves to purchase (see Fig. 4.4.).

You can open the sale by making an initial statement about the products you sell, or if you are uncertain about your prospect's needs, lead with an 'open' question. For example, a sales representative from a training organization may open with: 'How could your staff training be improved?' Generally, open questions start with one of the following words:

Who...?   *Why...?*   *What...?*
When...?   *Where...?*   *How...?*

The open question encourages the prospect to talk about their business. It gets them involved and interested from the start. It is your opportunity to begin to establish the need.

Never lead with a closed question – you may not like the response. For example, 'are you happy with the service your present suppliers give?' – if the prospect replies 'yes' then you have perhaps just reached an embarrassing end to the interview! Closed questions have their place in confirming needs, controlling the interview and guiding the prospect along a pathway of reasoning which will result in a successful close. For example:

Sales person: 'How could your staff training be improved?' (open question)
Prospect: 'The problem with using existing training courses at the local college, as we do at present, is that they are too general and the attendance times are often inconvenient.'
Sales person: 'So, your company would benefit from a tailor-made package, shaped to your specific training needs?' (closed question – to confirm and underline first need/problem)
Prospect: 'Yes.'
Sales person: 'And, it is also important that training takes place at a time and place that suits you?' (closed question – to confirm the second key need)
Prospect: 'Yes.'

In this simple example the sales person opened well. The first open question led to finding out two key needs. The following closed questions not only confirmed the problem but broke it down. Notice that the sales person resisted combining the two closed questions into one. Double questions can not only confuse the prospect, they can make it look like you are 'lecturing to them'. Short and to the point closed questions are better. They keep the prospect involved in the interview and order their thoughts in the way you want them to 'travel'.

However, you must at all costs avoid turning the interview into an interrogation. Both the prospect and yourself must feel at ease. A prospect who does not 'open up' may be encouraged further without it seeming like an interrogation by using simple prompts such as:

'And?'
'Really?'
'Why is that?'
'Could you explain a little further?'

or simply by use of controlled silence to denote they should continue. These short open-ended questions will invariably get even the quiet or awkward prospects to open up.

Once you are sure you have isolated the prospect's needs

you can offer the solution. This should be done using the 'point out the features sell the benefits' approach. This is where your (see earlier section *Product and service decisions*) features-benefits analysis pays off!

Closing the sale

Many ask the question: 'When should I start the attempt to close the sale?' The simple answer is that the close starts at the beginning of the sales interview. It is the logical result of a well-researched, planned and conducted interview.

The inexperienced approach the close with fear, apprehension and uncertainty. This is the bit which they think will turn the prospect against them and sour the rapport they have built up through the interview. The problem is lack of confidence. If you have done your job properly the prospect will want you to close, they will want their problem solved! Often the prospect will indicate that the time for your close is ripe by asking closed questions such as:

'What is the extent of your after-sales service?'
'What is the minimum order quantity?'
'How frequently can you deliver?'
'In what sizes and colours?'
'What discount do you offer on bulk purchases?'

Questions such as these tend to indicate they are more than interested, they want to buy! Don't miss the opportunity to close when it is handed to you! *Have confidence, be enthusiastic!*

In attempting to close you will undoubtedly come across objections. Some will be genuine, some merely excuses for not buying and others the result of misunderstanding.

Genuine objections occur where there is definite mismatch with what you are selling and what the prospect wants. If this is the case then even though you will not make the sale you can still gain a positive outcome by helping the prospect find the solution to their problem with another company. Even if this means giving a competitor business the long-term benefit to you is the trust that ensues. The prospect may buy something else from you at another time. They are also likely to tell others about you. They may also recommend to you another company.

Misunderstandings are the easiest to rectify. However, if you come across many objections of this type it would seem to indicate that there is something wrong with your overall style and technique – identify what is wrong and take action.

If you have correctly identified the prospect's problem and motivation, offered the right incentives to buy, communicated them well, then any objections the prospect puts in your path we can correctly identify as 'false' or 'excuses' for not buying. These can and should be overcome. False objections should never be addressed directly. They should be turned into reasons why the prospect should buy For example:

- Counter price objections with value for money/benefit statements, such as:

  'Even though our quote is higher than your present supplier, if you install our equipment what is your estimate of the savings you will make on wastage reduction in the first year?'

and attempt to close after the prospect has responded with:

  'Now doesn't that mean doing business with us makes more sense over the longer term?'

- Other objections relating to such factors as frequency of delivery, quality, reputation can be countered in similar ways. A small business may lack reputation, and be viewed as unreliable. The counter to this is that you can offer the prospect a quick and personal response to any problems. Refer them to testimonials from other customers.

Many prospects raise 'false objections' when they have to make a decision which will directly affect their success or failure within a company. You must reassure the prospect that they are making the right decision. The key is to identify and understand the prospect's personal motivations. It helps if you know who they are accountable to and for what.

Summary

The marketing plan can only be put together after extensive research of:

1. Why your customers buy and who they are.

2. The competition.
3. The threats and opportunities posed by the wider business environment.
4. Your own strengths and weaknesses.

This information, researched and developed in this and the previous two chapters, allows you to develop a detailed marketing plan within the marketing mix framework of:

Product
Price
Place
Promotion

Your decisions in each of these areas will add up to a unique selling proposition. This will represent what your business is and where it is going.

Advertising, sales promotion and personal selling are just the visible part of the marketing effort. Marketing starts with developing a product or service that the customer wants. In this way the sales person never ends up trying to sell a product nobody wants to buy.

Effective selling starts from the recognition that the sales person's job is to solve the customer's problem. Selling is a skill which can be learnt. Marketing is something that pervades the whole business.

It is well worth remembering:

● The first point of contact with a customer, whether it be face to face, on the telephone or by letter, makes a lasting impression.
● Where you are not selling a unique product (few businesses do) then it is the type or level of service provided that often clinches the sale.
● Customers buy benefits not products.
● Advertising, sales promotion and personal selling can be planned around the useful AIDA framework of Attention, Desire, Interest and Action.

5

premises

Calculating space requirement • Factors to consider when choosing a location • Buy or lease? • Planning permission and licences • Checklist and summary

Unless you plan to run your business from home you will need premises. Two of the key decisions that have to be made in acquiring premises is how big they should be and where they should be located. The size of your market and where it is located (see Chapter 3) and how it can be reached will have implications for your selection criteria for this asset.

Calculating space requirements

You should take great care in calculating your space requirements for selling, storage and/or manufacture as once decided upon and acquired they can prove difficult and costly to alter in the future. Careful thought should also be given to the future expansion rate: will the selling/storage and/or manu-facturing space be adequate to cope with your future plans?

The volume of physical sales will largely determine your space requirements. How many square feet you are liable to need for a given level of sales depends on what type of business you are in. Reference to government and trade statistics will often provide valuable indicators. For instance, statistics list the average sales per square foot for different types and sizes of retail operations. Given that you have an estimate of your turnover for your first year's trading, you can easily use this information to calculate your minimum space requirements (see Fig. 5.1).

Other types of business may need more complex approaches, involving the consideration of a number of variables. For instance, in a restaurant the pressure exerted on selling space is a combination of projected number of meals to be sold and number of sittings possible in a given time period. This will in turn dictate the number of tables and chairs required and hence the selling space needed. If a restaurant needs to cater for 72 meals during its peak period from 8pm to 10.30pm and the average length of service time per table is 50 minutes, then the number of sittings possible will be three (i.e. 150 min [length of peak perido] /50 min [service time]). Therefore, the number of seats that will be required will be: number of meals projected to be sold, 72/number of sittings, 3 = 24.

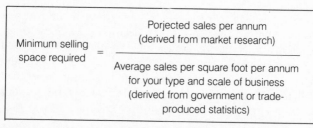

$$\text{Minimum selling space required} = \frac{\text{Porjected sales per annum (derived from market research)}}{\text{Average sales per square foot per annum for your type and scale of business (derived from government or trade-produced statistics)}}$$

Fig. 5.1 Using sales per square foot statistics to estimate selling space requirements

If the owner intends to have four seats per table then obviously six tables will be required. Assuming an allowance of 40 square feet for each table (including access) then the minimum space requirement for this restaurant will be 240 square feet (6 tables × 40 square feet [square foot requirement per table]).

➤ *Identify what will determine your selling space requirements. Will it be one or a combination of the following: number of customers expected in a given period; the time it takes to complete an individual sale; the physical size of your products; special needs of customers (e.g. extra space requirements for the disabled, extra wide shopping aisles for mothers with prams, etc.) Calculate the minimum and maximum size of selling space you will need.*

Manufacturing and administration space requirements will also be affected by volume of business. However, they will be modified by what plant and equipment you intend to acquire and what work organization you have. What is important is that early on in the planning of your business you should sketch out scale drawings of the optimum way of siting the necessary equipment.

Most businesses will need storage space for stock and raw materials. For those that trade in large volumes of physical stock, storage space will be directly determined by the stock levels maintained. In turn, the size of stock levels will be dictated by two factors: the sales level they will have to support and the frequency of deliveries you can secure.

Factors to consider when choosing a location

There may be a number of premises of the right size to choose from, but will they be in the right place? Usually the characteristics of your target markets, normally their various locations, will provide the key for deciding where to locate your premises. However, there are other considerations that should be weighed in the balance when deciding where to locate. For instance, the nature of your product or service might require the close proximity and availability of skilled labour, back-up services, stock and raw materials suppliers. The scale of the finance available to you may preclude city centre and main road locations. Your goal of a rapid growth rate might make some areas of good but relatively static growth undesirable.

➤ *Think very carefully about what your business will need in terms of location. Draw up a list of locational criteria by assessing the applicability and importance of the following factors to your business:*

1. Geographical concentrations of your market(s) – the pertinent question here is: will your customers come to you or will you go to them? If your customers are going to come to you, then obviously you will need to be located as close to them as possible. If you will be going to your customers, then your premises will have to be located for easy access to efficient road, rail and air networks for sale and distribution of your goods/services.

2. The needs and buying behaviour of your customers – in the course of your market research you should have identified the needs of your customers and translated them into the benefits your business should provide to fulfil those needs. What locational attributes should your business premises have to cater for your customers' needs and buying behaviour? For example, convenience might dictate that your premises should be close to a system of transport your customers use (e.g. bus routes and bus stops, car parking facilities, etc.). In some product and service markets, customers habitually shop around before making a buying decision, good examples being female fashion and estate agents. Therefore, if your markets display similar buying behaviour, you should find premises that are in the same area as your competition. In this way the cluster of similar businesses can act as a magnet, drawing customers in.

3. The image of your product/service – the area in which you locate must be consistent with the overall image of your business. A retailer of designer clothes would probably lack credibility trading in a run-down inner-city area.

4. Evidence of market decline in a locality – a number of vacant premises or businesses for sale in the area should raise serious doubts about the potential of such a location. What has gone wrong? Find out.

5. Future changes to a location that might affect trade – the ideally located premises that you have found might not be as attractive in the future when the bus route is moved, parking restrictions are imposed in front of your premises and the new road cuts off your passing trade.

Buy or lease

There is no 'right answer' to this one, it is a matter for you to decide in relation to your business's requirements. Here are some of the factors to consider.

Buying a freehold property is a major capital investment. The main disadvantage is obvious: you will have to find the finance (see Chapter 8) for the purchase. The repayments and cost of that finance will probably prove to be more than outgoings associated with a leasehold purchase. However, you will be buying an asset that will appreciate in value and thus in future years it should provide a sound base for raising further finance for expansion. With the purchase of a lease, the opposite is true; as the years on the lease are used up, it will depreciate in value. Further, because of the lack of permanence with a lease and the fact that it decreases in value, you will find it more difficult to raise finance for its acquisition. The opposite is true for freehold property: you will find a range of financial institutions prepared to make long-term loans on such an investment.

Generally, you will find that there are more constraints and controls attached to the operation of a business from a leasehold than freehold premises. Both will, of course, be subject to planning permission, but the leasehold agreement is more than likely to contain clauses imposing repair and maintenance obligations, and restrictions on uses and alterations.

Planning permission and licences

The golden rule here is to double-check that the premises you intend to acquire can in fact be used for all the activities you intend to carry out now and, just as important, in the future. This is just as true with the purchase of an existing business.

The main categories of use are:

- retail
- office
- light industrial
- general industrial

Within each broad category there are further sub-divisions. In the first instance, check with your local authority planning office and later in detail with your solicitor. You should also note that you will need planning permission for any alterations, including new shop fronts and signs. Further, most alterations and extensions will have to conform to building regulations. The main thing to note here is that seeking such permission can be a lengthy and sometimes costly process. You will certainly need legal advice and more than likely the services of an architect and surveyor.

You must also check with your local authority whether the existence of any local by-laws will impose any restrictions or controls on your business. A licence, registration or other permissions may also be needed (see Chapter 9).

Checklist and summary

For many, in particular retail businesses, acquisition of the right premises is perhaps one of the most important decisions ever made in a business career. Use the following checklist to help you make sure you have got it right.

1. Have you calculated your present and future space requirements?
2. Which of the following are important factors in determining best location (rank them in order to use as a checking list):
   - Closeness to customers' homes, places of work, etc.
   - Parking facilities.
   - Transport facilities for customers.
   - Proximity to competitors (i.e. your customers like to shop around).
   - Proximity to other customer magnets (e.g. banks, large stores, bus stops, sunny side of the street, main shopping areas, etc.).
   - Cheap and efficient access to suppliers.
   - Proximity to labour force.
   - Image of area.
   - Other...?
3. Have you severe restrictions on the amount you can borrow?
4. If so, have you considered a lease instead of freehold?
5. Or a different form of distribution (see Chapter 4)?
6. If buying a lease, have you:
   - Obtained legal advice?
   - Checked that the present owner has the right to sell the lease?
   - Checked all the details of the lease?
   - The rent might be acceptable now, but a fundamental aspect of – leases are rent reviews – have you discussed this with your solicitor?
   - Checked the attitude of financial institutions to your borrowing requirements for such a lease?
   - Other...?

7. Have you obtained planning permission?
8. Have you taken into account any future uses your business may put the property to as it expands?
9. If buying freehold, are there any covenants in the deeds which will pose a threat to your business?
10. How easily will you be able to find a buyer for the premises if the business fails?
11. Have you checked whether any local by-laws apply?
12. Have you calculated the full cost of the premises:
    – legal fees for buying, planning permission, licence applications, etc.
    – surveying fees
    – cost of finance
    – advance rent
    – rates
    – alterations and improvements
    – costs of conforming with environmental health, and health and safety regulations
    – insurances
    – service connection charges
    – if already in business, costs to disturbance of business (loss of sales, etc.)
    – other...?

6

will you make a profit?

Your costs • The break-even point: sales volume, costs, selling price and profit • The projected profit and loss accoun • Summary • Checklist

The previous chapter should have helped you establish the scale of demand for your product or service and a range of prices potential customers might be prepared to pay. The next step is to establish whether the costs involved in exploiting the market will result in a large enough profit to warrant investigating the business idea further.

The solution to the problem is at first sight simple. Reasonably, you may think it is a matter of establishing the revenue you will earn from your market and deducting all the costs in selling and/or producing your product/service. To see whether this is true, let's take an imaginary example of a business making and selling widgets. To keep the example simple, the business has two costs: rent and equipment costs per annum of £10 000 and a raw material cost of £1.00 per widget. The business has estimated it will sell 20 000 widgets in its first year's trading. With a prevailing market price of £2.00 it sets out to estimate its profit:

Sales volume revenue (20 000 × £2.00):	£10 000	£40 000
Rent and equipment costs:	£10 000	
Raw materials costs (20 000 × £1.00):	£20 000	
Total costs:		£30 000
Profit:		£10 000

The business will be profitable, or will it? What will happen if the sales drop by half? Will this result in the profits being halved to £5000? The answer is no, because not all of the costs have the same characteristics. Logically the raw materials cost will be reduced by half in proportion with the drop in sales – not as many raw materials need to be purchased. But what about the other costs? The business will still have to pay rent on the premises and maintain its equipment regardless of how many it sells – these costs will remain the same. The business will not be profitable:

Sales revenue (10 000 × £2.00):	£10 000	£20 000
Rent and equipment costs:	£10 000	
Raw materials costs (10 000 × £1.00):	£10 000	
Total costs:		£20 000
Profit:		Zero!

You should be able to see that for this business to operate at a profit it would have to do one or a combination of the following:

(a) Increase its sales volume
(b) Increase the selling price
(c) Reduce its costs

However, attempts to change one factor to the advantage of the business may inadvertently bring about a disastrous change in another. For example, if the selling price of widgets is increased to £2.50 in an attempt to offset the effect of the fall in sales, customers may go elsewhere to seek cheaper prices, possibly cutting the already reduced sales volume by half. This would put the business in an even worse position:

Sales revenue (5 000 × £2.50):		£12 500
Rent and equipment costs:	£10 000	
Raw materials costs (5 000 × £1.00):	£5 000	
Total costs:		£15 000
Loss:		£2 500

This very simple example clearly shows that the task of estimating profit is not as simple as it first appears. The factors that determine profit – costs, sales volume and selling price – are all intertwined. Altering one factor can have a marked effect on one or all of the others.

To be able to predict the profit or loss your business venture could make, we need some method or model capable of clearly calculating and showing the impact of changes in any one of these factors on the profitability of your intended business. We require a model that will answer all those 'if, what questions', such as: 'if I fail to meet my sales target by 10% what will my total profits be!' or 'if my stock costs rise by 15% how many more do I need to sell to maintain my profits?' and so on. To build up this model we will have to examine all of its components – cost, selling price, sales volume – in much more detail.

Your costs

Not all expenditure is a cost!

Before proceeding to examine the characteristics and structure of costs in detail, it is important for you to understand what is and what isn't a cost to a business. Otherwise you may fall into the trap of classifying all the expenditure you make in relation to your business as a cost.

Money going into a business is soaked up into two distinct areas, the costs the business incurs and its capital requirements (for a full discussion of the characteristics of capital, see Chapter 7). To be able to easily distinguish between expenditure on costs and capital, you would be well advised to remember the following working definitions:

> **Cost** is the value of something the business has used.
> **Capital** is the value of something the business has.

To illustrate, if a business buys in £20 000 worth of stock at the beginning of the month and has £5000 worth left at the end of the month, then £15 000 of stock will have been sold (discounting the possibility of theft and wastage). This, having been used up in the business, will be a cost, while the £5000 of stock left on the shelves, being something the business has, will be capital.

➤ *Try to determine which items from the following list of expenditure made by a taxi proprietor in his first year represent capital investment in the business and which are definitely costs:*

	£
Car	5500
Fare meter	500
Expenditure on maintenance	1000
Petrol and oil	3000

You would be right to identify the expenditure on maintenance charges, petrol and the oil as costs, for those items will have been used up by the business in the course of the year. On the other hand, you cannot count all of the expenditure on the car and the fare meter as a cost because the taxi proprietor will still possess both items at the end of the year. However, it is obvious that the car and the meter, through their use in the business, will have lost value – they will have depreciated. The amount by which they have depreciated can be counted as a cost.

The important thing to remember is that the cost of major capital purchases (known as fixed assets) are spread out over their working life. For example, a van costing £8000 with an expected working life of four years could be depreciated at £2000 per annum.

When finance has been secured to acquire major items, newcomers to business often make the mistake of double-counting the cost by counting both loan repayments and the depreciation as a cost to the business. The loan repayment is not a cost to the business, it is simply a repayment of capital and as such it must come out of profits. However, any fees connected with arranging the finance and interest payable are costs.

To determine what depreciation costs your business will incur, you will need to identify what your major purchases will be (see Chapter 7) and then adopt a suitable method of providing for depreciation. You may care to use the next section to select a method or decide to leave it to your accountant.

Methods of providing for depreciation

There are a number of ways of providing for depreciation of assets. Here we will briefly consider three of the most popular.

- straight-line method
- the production hour method
- reducing balance method

All of the following methods allocate the same total amount for depreciation, i.e. the full cost of the purchase less resale value (if any). It is timing of the costs that differentiates each method.

The straight-line method seeks to spread the cost of the asset evenly over its working life. As it is simple to work out, it is commonly used, but only really suitable for assets whose resale value declines with time and not usage. The calculation for determining annual depreciation is:

$$\frac{\text{Original cost (or revaluation)} - \text{Resale value}}{\text{Working life (years)}}$$

For example, if a cold store cabinet is bought for £4000 with a planned life with the business of four years and an estimated resale value of £2000, then the annual rate of depreciation will be £500.

The production hour method is more suitable for assets such as machinery whose resale value may be largely determined by how many hours (or miles, etc.) they have been worked. The calculation again is simple:

$$\frac{\text{Depreciation}}{\text{per hour}} = \frac{\text{Original cost (or revaluation)} - \text{Resale value}}{\begin{array}{c}\text{Working life in units of usage}\\ \text{(e.g. hours, miles, etc.)}\end{array}}$$

For example, if a machine is bought for £20,000 with a planned working life of 80,000 hours, then the hourly depreciation would be £0.25. If the machine is operated for 160 hours in one month, then the monthly depreciation cost will be £40.00.

Both of the above methods fail to take into account the

1. Enter the residual value
2. Press divide
3. Enter the original cost or revaluation
4. Press the equals key
5. Press the log key
6. Press divide
7. Enter the useful life of asset
8. Press the equals key
9. Press inv (invert) and then the log key (to obtain the anti log)
10. Press multiply
11. Enter 100 and press equals
12. Finally subtract the answer from 100

Fig. 6.1 Using a calculator to obtain the annual percentage rate of depreciation (reducing balance)

commonly known fact that many assets can lose a higher proportion of their second-hand value in their early life. You will have no doubt recognized this in the many domestic purchases you have made: cars, TVs, washing machines etc. The reducing balance method seeks to take this into account by attributing larger depreciation costs in the earlier years. This is done by decreasing the value of the asset by a fixed percentage each year. The result is to allocate costs on a 'diminishing sliding scale' as time goes by. However, using this method, the value of an asset is never reduced to zero!

$$\text{Annual percentage rate of depreciation} = 1 - \sqrt[4]{\frac{£2000}{£4000}} \times 100$$

$$= 15.9\%$$

	Reducing balance method Depreciation:			Straight-line method Depreciation:		
Yr end	Net value	Annual	Cumulative	Net value	Annual	Cumulative
Start	4000	–	–	4000	–	–
1	3364	636	636	3500	500	500
2	2829	535	1171	3000	500	1000
3	2379	450	1621	2500	500	1500
4	2000	379	2000	2000	500	2000

Fig. 6.2 The reducing balance and straight-line methods compared

The formula for calculating the percentage rate to be used is.

$$\frac{\text{Annual percentage}}{\text{rate of depreciation}} = 1 - n\sqrt{\frac{\text{Residual value}}{\text{Cost}}} \times 100$$

Note: n is the useful life of the asset.

This calculation looks difficult but is relatively simple with a modern calculator that has logarithm capability. You don't have to understand why the calculation works but only how to operate it. On most calculators, the procedure is as clearly laid out in Fig. 6.1. If you have got such a calculator, try to apply the reducing balance method on the information in our cold store cabinet example – you will find the solution and the comparison of the methods in Fig. 6.2.

The reducing balance method may be more complicated to calculate but for many assets it will better reflect reality. It evens out the asset's operating costs over time by counterbalancing the decline in depreciation by the increasing maintenance costs as the asset becomes worn with usage.

In selecting your method you must give careful consideration to the type of asset and how it will lose value. In the end you may wish to ignore the above methods and calculate the depreciation of your assets on sound estimates of their resale value after each year's trading periods. Whichever method you choose, you should be aware that the Inland Revenue lay down varying rates of depreciation (capital allowances) for different types of assets. Therefore, before they calculate your tax bill they will alter your depreciation figure (for more information on taxation, see Chapter 9).

➤ *Now using a table similar to that in Fig. 6.3 estimate your fixed asset costs.*

So far we have identified what defines a cost and looked in detail at one kind of cost depreciation. There are, of course, many other costs involved in operating a business and, as discussed at the beginning of the chapter, certain costs react in different ways to changes in sales volume. We must now

item	Total cost (£)	Life (yrs)	Depreciation first yr (£)	Comments
1.				
2.				
3.				
4.				
5.				
Total capital		Total first yr		

Fig. 6.3 Charting the cost of your fixed assets

turn our attention to classifying the costs involved in running your business.

Fixed costs

These are the costs you will have to pay whether your business is doing well or badly. A good test to apply to determine whether an item is a fixed cost is to ask the question, 'If I don't sell anything at all will I still have to pay out for this item?' If you will, then it is definitely a fixed cost. For example, a shop will have to pay items such as rent, electricity, and permanent staff wages even if no customers come into the shop! Over short periods of time, say less than a year, these costs will change very little with how much you sell – they are 'fixed' and not affected by changes in sales volume. Obviously, over a longer period they may change as you take on more staff, buy extra machinery or move to larger premises.

We can now start to build our model of how costs, sales volume, selling price and profit interact together by drawing up a simple chart to show how fixed costs behave in relation to sales volume (Fig. 6.4).

Variable costs

These are costs that vary with changes in sales volume – hence their name *variable*. Their key characteristic is that they will rise or fall in direct proportion with rises or falls in sales volume. For most businesses the main variable cost will

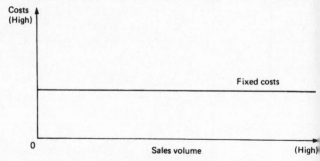

Fig. 6.4 Sales volume and fixed costs

be raw materials and other stocks. It can be easily seen that these will vary in direct proportion with how much is sold or manufactured.

We can now build our model one step further by graphing how variable costs change with sales volume (Fig. 6.5).

Costs and sales volume

Now we can bring both types of cost together and see how unit cost (that is the cost of selling/producing each product) is affected by sales volume. Let's take a simple example to illustrate the effect.

Hifas is a small business producing and selling knitwear. Its fixed costs for one year of trading are estimated at £10 000 and the cost of materials to make one jumper (its unit variable cost) is £2.00. Hifas's total variable costs will,

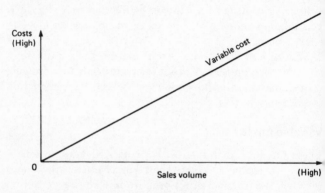

Fig. 6.5 Sales volume and variable costs

of course, vary for different levels of sales: 15 000 sales will result in £30 000 variable costs; £5000 sales will cost £10 000, and so on. Figure 6.6 shows the relationship between its fixed and variable costs over a range of sales levels.

The total cost of producing each sale can easily be calculated from Fig. 6.6 by dividing total costs for a given level of sales by the number sold. Let's have a look at the total unit cost for a range of sales volumes:

Sales	Total cost £	Unit cost £
5 000	20 000	4.00
10 000	30 000	3.00
15 000	40 000	2.66

You can see that for higher sales levels the cost of producing and selling each item is reduced. The variable cost per unit will remain the same but the fixed costs per unit are reduced as they are spread out over a greater output (i.e. total fixed costs divided by output = unit fixed costs):

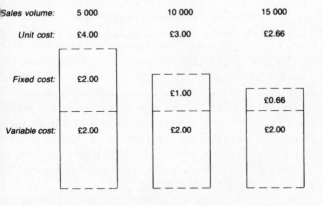

Sales volume:	5 000	10 000	15 000
Unit cost:	£4.00	£3.00	£2.66
Fixed cost:	£2.00	£1.00	£0.66
Variable cost:	£2.00	£2.00	£2.00

The cost of each unit of sale obviously sets a bottom line on the price you can charge and still make a profit. If the highest price Hifas could set is £3.00, then it would certainly make a profit with 15 000 sales per annum but quite a large loss if there were only 5000 sales. At a sales level of 10 000 units it would neither make a loss nor a profit – this is known as its break-even point. It is critical for any business

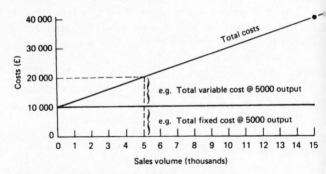

Fig. 6.6 Sales volume, fixed and variable costs

to know this point, when sales revenue will begin to overtake costs and produce a profit.

The break-even point:
sales volume, costs, selling price and profit

We can now add selling price to our model to complete the picture of how the sales volume, cost and selling price interact to produce a profit or loss. Let's continue with our knitwear example and add the sales revenue line to the graph of sales volume and costs. To do this, first we have to select a possible selling price, say £4.00, multiply it by a selected output, say 10 000 units (to give a sales revenue for that level of sales, £40000), and mark this point on the graph. Secondly, as the sales revenue will rise and fall in direct proportion with rises and falls in sales, all we need to do is to take a ruler and draw a line from the point of zero revenue) through the point we have just marked on the graph. The result is shown in Fig. 6.7.

The point where the sales revenue line intersects the total costs line is where the business will just be making sufficient revenue to cover all costs: this is the BEP (break-even point). Below that sales volume, the business will make a loss: above, it will make a profit. Drawing the graph helps you to quickly see and read off the various profits or losses you could make at any given level of sales.

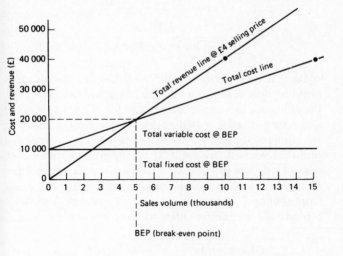

Fig. 6.7 Sales volume, costs, sales revenue and profit

➤ *Try it for yourself: take a sheet of graph paper and redraw Fig. 6.7. What profit or loss will Hifas make at the following sales volumes: 3000, 7000, 12 000, 14 000?*

You can turn the graph into a more dynamic model by adding different sales revenue lines to gauge the effect of different selling prices.

➤ *What will the break-even points be for the following selling prices: £3.50, £3.00, £2.50? In other words, how much more in each case would Hifas have to sell to break even on these reduced selling prices? Add the new revenue lines to your graph to find out.*

Gross profit and break-even

As we have just seen, we can work out the BEP by drawing a graph. We can also use a formula to achieve the same ends:

$$BEP = \frac{Fixed}{Unit\ selling\ price - Unit\ variable\ cost}$$

Unit selling price minus unit variable cost gives the gross profit per unit of sale. For example, if you are selling records, the difference between what you pay for one (its cost price) and what you sell it at (selling price) is the amount you have left over to pay fixed costs and hopefully retain some net profit for yourself (see Fig. 6.8). As the gross profit on each item of sale has to *contribute* to the payment of the fixed costs, you will have to make enough individual gross profits (contributions) to cover fixed costs to break even. The above formula can thus be simplified to:

$$BEP = \frac{Gross\ profit}{Fixed\ costs}$$

Let's substitute some figures from our example to demonstrate. With a selling price of £4.00 and variable costs of £2.00, Hifas makes a gross profit of £2.00 per unit of sale. As we know its fixed costs are £10 000, it will have to sell 5000 items to cover its fixed costs and break even (5000 × £2.00 unit gross profit = £10 000).

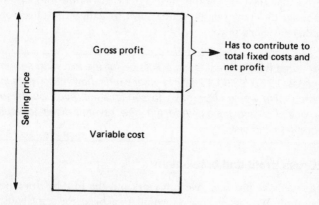

Fig. 6.8 The Structure of a cost

➤ *To gain some experience in using the formula, check the answers that you obtained from the graph with the formula.*

Multi-product break-even

We have now created the model we started at the beginning of the chapter, but the probability is that it will not fit the requirements of your intended business. We have created a model that only deals with a business selling one kind of product, which is very rare. In this section we will consider a number of methods for calculating the break-even sales point for businesses selling a range of different products. The first method offers a simple solution where the percentage profit margin can be derived from published statistics. The second method is more complex but provides more information in giving break-even sales figures for individual products or product groups by allocating fixed costs on the proportion of total gross profits each product is expected to earn.

Both methods are explained with the use of comprehensive examples. You would be well advised to have a calculator on hand to enable you to follow them through and thereby improve your understanding.

Method 1: Using the gross profit percentage margin

If you are running a shop you could be selling hundreds, if not thousands, of different products. How can you calculate the break-even point for such a business? The answer is perhaps simpler than you may think. Retail businesses common to a particular type, such as newsagents and small grocery stores, tend to operate to a set gross profit margin (see Fig. 7.5). This is because they tend to sell in similar markets and buy in stock at similar cost prices. The gross profit margin, simply being the gross profit expressed as a percentage of the sales, can thus be substituted in the BEP formula for actual gross profit:

$$BEP = \frac{\text{Fixed cost}}{\text{\% gross margin}}$$

For example, a small grocery store with an expected margin

of 20% and fixed costs of £10 000 per annum would calculate its break-even point as follows:

$$BEP = \frac{£10\ 000}{20\%\ (\text{i.e. } 20/100)}$$

$$BEP = \frac{£10\ 000}{0.2}$$

$$BEP = £50\ 000$$

This too can be shown in graph form. The graph is constructed as before but this time the variable cost and revenue line is omitted and replaced by a gross profit line. Figure 6.9 illustrates the break-even point for the small grocery store.

The gross profit line is drawn by first selecting a sales volume – £100 000 in the example – then calculating how much gross profit the volume of sales will produce with a given margin (20% in the example) – in this case it will be 20% of £100 000 which is £20 000 gross profit – and

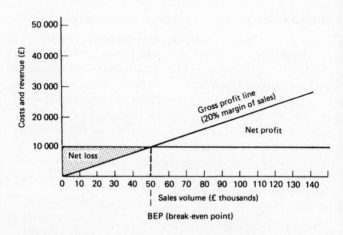

Fig. 6.9 Constructing a break-even chart using a gross profit margin

marking the profit against the level of sales on the graph. The gross profit line is then drawn with a ruler from zero gross profit/zero sales (obviously, zero sales will result in zero profit) through the marked point on the graph. You can see that the graph gives the same sales, £50 000, to break even as the formula method does.

➤ *Try constructing your own graph. The business may not be able to achieve the break-even sales figure. What sales figure would it have to achieve to break even if it charged slightly higher prices and operated on a 25% margin?*

➤ *To give you some more practice, let's presume the business faces higher stock costs and therefore has to operate on a reduced margin of 15%. With a 15% margin, what is the new BEP? What sales level will have to be achieved to make a net profit of £10 000?*

Note: *You can either construct a graph and plot all of the different gross profit lines (i.e. 15%, 20% and 25%) or use the formula. Work with the method you find the easiest.*

Method 2: Allocating fixed costs to each product on the basis of gross profit earned

If you intend to sell/produce a range of products all with different profit margins and no published or accepted percentage margin to use as a guide, you can still use the break-even formula. You have to decide on some method of apportioning the fixed costs to each product or product group. There are a number of ways of doing this. One, not unreasonable, method is to allocate fixed costs to each product on the basis of the percentage of total gross profits each is expected to generate. Simply, a product that generates more gross profit than another will be called upon to 'pay' a larger share of the overheads. However, do not mistake a large profit margin on a product as an indicator that it will produce the largest gross profit. It is the number of times that profit margin is earned (sales × profit margin) that is important. It is better to sell 10 000 items at a penny profit per item than 10 items at £1 profit per item!

Although in the planning stage you cannot fully forecast

the sales of each product, you can estimate the percentage of total sales of each product. In other words, your market research should be able to tell you which product you are likely to sell the most of and which the least. As you can also estimate your variable cost and the selling price, you can also calculate your gross profit margin on each product. Having collected this information you are now in a position to allocate overheads on the basis of the proportion of total profits each product is expected to produce. For example, if you intend to sell two products, A and B, with respective profit margins of 30% and 40%, and product A is expected to sell three times as much as product B, so that A will generate 75% of the sales and B 25%, then fixed costs would be allocated to each product by calculating the ratio (proportion) of A : B in providing total gross profit, as follows:

	Sales	×	Margin	= Gross profit
A:	75	×	30	= 2250
B:	25	×	40	= 1000

This gives a ratio of 2250:1000, simplified by cancelling down to 9:4. Therefore fixed costs will be apportioned:

9/13 × 100 = 69.23% to product A
4/13 × 100 = 30.77% to product B

With overheads of £1000, £692 will be allocated to A and £308 to B. The break-even can then be calculated using the standard formula: BEP = Fixed costs/Gross margin. Which would be £2306 for product A and £770 for product B, giving a total break-even sales figure for the business of £3075. The same result can be achieved by modifying the standard break-even formula to include the above information:

$$BEP = \frac{\text{Fixed costs}}{\underset{(\%S \times P)}{\text{Product A}} + \underset{(\%S \times P)}{\text{Product B}}}$$

$$BEP = \frac{£1000}{(0.75 \times 0.30) + (0.25 \times 0.4)}$$

$$\text{BEP} = \frac{£1000}{0.225 + 0.1}$$

$$\text{BEP} = \frac{£1000}{0.325}$$

$$\text{BEP} = £3076$$

Let's take a more realistic example to explore the process in more detail. Southern Fried (an imaginary business), a fast-food outlet, plans to sell three products: chicken burger, standard chicken and family bucket. They have researched the market and costs, and the selling prices and variable costs are as follows:

	Chicken burger	Standard chicken	Family bucket
Selling price:	1.00	2.00	4.00
Variable cost	0.50	1.50	2.40
Gross profit (contribution):	0.50	0.50	1.60
Percentage margin (profit/selling price × 100):	50%	25%	40%

Southern Fried don't expect to sell the products in equal amounts. Market research estimates that the business's total £ sales for the coming year will be made up as follows:

30% of £ sales will be in chicken burgers
50% of £ sales will be in standard chickens
20% of £ sales will be in family buckets

Southern Fried's fixed costs are estimated at £10000 per annum.

To calculate the total sales needed to break even, Southern Fried use an extended version of the break-even formula:

$$\text{BEP} = \frac{\text{Fixed cost}}{\underset{(\%S \times P)}{\text{Product X}} + \underset{(\%S \times P)}{\text{Product Y}} + \underset{(\%S \times P)}{\text{Product Z}}}$$

Notes:

X = chicken burgers
Y = standard chicken
Z = family buckets
%S = percentage of total sales in each product
P = gross profit (contribution) produced by the product

● If the sales percentage represents physical units of sale, then the gross profit must be expressed in money. Accordingly, the break-even sales figure will be in physical units.
● If the sales percentage represents £ sales, then the gross profit figure must be expressed as a percentage margin. Accordingly, the break-even sales figure will be in pounds.

Using the formula we can obtain the total sales in pounds Southern Fried needs to break even:

$$BEP = \frac{£10\ 000}{(0.3 \times 0.5) + (0.5 \times 0.25) + (0.2 \times 0.4)}$$

$$= \frac{£10\ 000}{0.355}$$

$$= £28\ 169$$

As we already know what percentage of total sales will be in each product, we can easily calculate the break-even sales (£) for each product. In addition, to prove the 'external formula' works, let's calculate the gross profit each product will contribute to fixed costs to see whether it is sufficient:

Product	% of total sales	Break-even sales (£)	Margin (%)	Gross profit
Burgers	30	8 451	50	4,226
Chicken	50	14 085	25	3 521
Family	20	5 633	40	2,253
	100%	£28 169		£10 000

To calculate the number that has to be sold is a simple matter of dividing sales by selling price for each product. In this case, Southern Fried would have to sell 8451 chicken burgers, 7042 chicken meals and 1408 family buckets in the coming year just to break even. This works out at 162 burgers, 135 standard chickens and 27 family buckets per week.

The calculations involved to achieve the break-even figure for this example seem tedious but with practice can be done quite quickly. If you build this multi-product break-even model using a computer spreadsheet you can substitute a range of selling prices and costs and recalculate the BEP with ease – this will greatly help decisions relating to prices, costs and sales mix.

When this calculation has been done once, you can easily obtain an overall percentage gross profit margin for the sales mix and transfer the information to a graph to study the effect on profits over a range of sales volumes. Southern Fried's expected gross margin from its sales mix is easily calculated by dividing BEP gross profit by BEP total sales and multiplying the result by 100, i.e. £10 000/£28 169 × 100 = 35.5% gross profit margin on sales.

The break-even profit point (BEPP)

We have already used the model to identify the profits that will be earned with varying combinations of sales volumes, costs and selling prices. However, it would be advantageous to start with a desired profit and proceed directly to calculate the level of sales required to achieve it. Calculation of the break-even profit point is simply a matter of adding your profit goal to fixed costs and dividing the result by the gross profit/contribution per unit of sale:

$$\text{BEPP} = \frac{\text{Fixed costs} + \text{Desired profits}}{\text{Unit gross profit}}$$

In other words, you are asking the question, 'how many individual contributions of gross profit will have to be made to cover both fixed costs and my desired profit?'

Suppose in our previous example the owners of Southern Fried had to meet a profit goal of £15 000, then the break-even profit point would be:

$$\text{BEPP} = \frac{£10\ 000 + £15\ 000}{35.5\% \text{ (i.e. } 35.5/100 = 0.355)}$$

$$\text{BEPP} = \frac{£25\ 000}{0.355}$$

$$\text{BEPP} = £70\ 423$$

As we already know the percentage of total sales in each product, you may like to work out BEPP for each product.

Estimating your target profit

As we have seen, if your estimates and classification of costs are accurate, you can use the break-even model to readily identify the sales volume necessary to generate a desired net profit. The unanswered question is what target profits should you be aiming for. The answer 'to make a living' is not simply enough, nor is some figure off the top of your head. Out of net profits you will have to provide for:

1. What you consider to be sufficient living expenses for yourself. You may use your present annual wage plus an allowance for inflation, but you must add on the non-wage benefits associated with employment, such as sick pay and pension schemes, which you will only receive at additional cost when you become self-employed.
2. Repayment of capital loans less interest.
3. Allowance for retaining some profits in the business to finance future capital requirements (see Chapter 7). Although the replacement of fixed assets is partly allowed for in the cost of depreciation, you would be well advised to remember that the replacement cost may be well in excess of original purchase price – you will have to find the difference out of profits or take on another capital loan. Many businesses face bankruptcy after their first few years because they have failed to allow for sufficient profits to be retained to finance further expansion.

   Further, you should be seeking a profit that represents a satisfactory return on the money invested in the business. The profits earned by your business should be greater than the return you would get if the money (yours or borrowed) was invested elsewhere, say a savings account. For example, with an interest rate of 10%, say, offered on savings accounts, £100 000 invested in a business should produce net profits well in excess of £10 000 per annum, otherwise the owner might as well stay in bed and put the money in the bank Further, while there is virtually no risk of not getting your money plus interest back from a savings account, an investment in a small business is fraught with risk. You should be aiming for profits that will represent a far higher return on capital invested than offered by a savings account. The riskier your business, the higher the rate of return on capital invested should be.

Calculate what your minimum profits per annum should be to represent a satisfactory return on your investment by:

● Finding out the current rate of interest (before tax) on savings accounts.
● Adding on a percentage for the element of risk involved. For an entirely new product this will be high (say 30%), for a tried and tested business this will be low (say 10%).
● Calculating the average capital that will be employed in the business over its trading year (see Chapter 7).
● Then using the following calculation:

Profit = Capital employed × Target percentage return

For example:

Capital to be employed:	£50 000
Current rate of interest:	10%
Provision for element of risk:	20%
Target rate of return on capital employed:	30%

Therefore, minimum profits per annum required to provide a satisfactory return on capital employed in the business: £50 000 × 30% (30/100) = £15 000.

Sales volume, profit and cost calculations for businesses dealing in unique products

Contribution per labour hour

Many small businesses are involved in providing a unique

product or service to each customer. For a plumber, no two jobs will be exactly the same, each will use up different amounts of labour and materials. This is true for many jobbing firms. In such cases a method is required for producing estimates that will realize sufficient gross profit to cover both target net profit and overheads.

The way to proceed is to identify what factor limits your sales volume: for most service firms, this is the number of labour hours in a given period. The next step is to calculate how much gross profit will have to be generated by each labour hour to cover the target profit and fixed costs. This is a simple matter of dividing fixed costs for the period by total labour hours available:

$$\text{Contribution required from each hour} = \frac{\text{Fixed costs + Net profit target}}{\text{Total labour hours available}}$$

For a garage with fixed costs of £400 (including staff wages) and a profit objective of £400 per week and 80 labour hours available, each labour hour would have to generate £10 gross profit for the business to break even. However, this assumes that all the labour hours the firm has paid wages for (assuming permanent staff are employed) have been used up – in most cases this is not so. Sales will fluctuate throughout the year – some weeks may see only 70% of the employees' time gainfully used. Therefore it is safer to substitute total labour hours available for a conservative estimate of total labour hours that will be directly used in generating gross profit:

$$\text{Contribution required from each hour} = \frac{\text{Fixed costs + Net profit target}}{\substack{\text{Total labour hours used} \\ \text{(conservative estimate)}}}$$

If we rework the previous example with a conservative estimate that on average only 75% of the total labour hours available will be used, then the contribution required per man hour will be £13.33 (i.e. £800/60 hours). On this basis the costing for a job might look like this:

Materials:	£44.50
Contribution to fixed costs and net profits, 10 hours @ £13.33 per hour:	£133.30
Total charge for job	£177.80

£177.80 is the price the business would have to charge for this job to cover all costs and meet its profit goal. If this is a higher price than the customer is prepared to pay, should the business accept less to secure the order? There is no simple answer to this question – the business will have to consider the following:

● Will turning down the job result in labour hours being idle?
● Will acceptance of the job result in profitable repeat sales?
● Will accepting the job take up slack labour hours?

If the answer to any of these questions is yes, accepting the order at a lower price would probably benefit the business. The lowest price that could be accepted is one that will at least cover fixed costs. Contribution required per hour could be reduced to £400/60 hours = £6.60. The lowest possible costing would therefore be:

Materials:	£44.50
Contribution to fixed costs and net profits, 10 hours £6.60 per hour:	£66.00
Total charge for job	£110.50

Provided more profitable business is not being turned down, the logic of charging a price that does not fully contribute to desired profits is that at least it earns some money towards fixed costs. Remember, fixed costs will not change if you sell less, they will continue to build up and have to be met by your remaining sales.

Cost plus profit markup – markups and margins

An alternative to the above method is to add a percentage to variable costs to obtain a selling price – this percentage is known as the markup. It should not be confused with the percentage profit margin. Although both refer to the same profit in money terms, in the case of profit margin the profit is expressed as a percentage of sales whereas in the case of markup it is expressed as a percentage of variable cost. The actual money markup (i.e. gross profit) per job or unit of production, when multiplied by the number of expected sales, will as before have to be high enough to cover target profit and fixed costs.

To decide on what percentage markup to apply, you must first identify a percentage profit margin that will give you an acceptable combination of sales volume, costs and net profit. This is achieved by plotting your fixed costs on a graph and drawing in different gross profit lines based on possible percentage margins (as in Fig. 6.9).

When you have decided on an acceptable percentage gross margin on sales you will need to convert this to its equivalent percentage markup to arrive at selling price for each job or unit of production. The process is as follows:

$$\text{Profit margin} = \frac{\text{Profit}}{\text{Price}}$$

$$\text{Profit markup} = \frac{\text{Profit}}{\text{Variable cost}}$$

Then the percentage markup can be derived from the percentage margin by the following process:

$$\text{Profit markup} = \frac{\text{Profit}}{\underset{\text{(i.e. variable cost)}}{\text{Price} - \text{Profit}}} \times 100 \text{ (to turn the fraction into a percentage)}$$

The process can be easily reversed to derive a percentage margin from a percentage markup:

$$\text{Profit markup} = \frac{\text{Profit}}{\underset{\text{(i.e. price)}}{\text{Variable cost} + \text{Profit}}} \times 100 \text{ (to turn the fraction into a percentage)}$$

For example, if you decided that operating a 20% gross profit margin on sales would give you the best chance of

Margin	Markup	Margin	Markup	Margin	Markup
1.00%	1.01%	34.00%	51.52%	67.00%	203.03%
2.00%	2.04%	35.00%	53.85%	68.00%	212.50%
3.00%	3.09%	36.00%	56.25%	69.00%	222.58%
4.00%	4.10%	37.00%	58.73%	70.00%	233.33%
5.00%	5.26%	38.00%	61.29%	71.00%	244.83%
6.00%	5.38%	39.00%	63.93%	72.00%	257.14%
7.00%	7.53%	40.00%	66.67%	73.00%	270.37%
8.00%	8.70%	41.00%	69.49%	74.00%	284.62%
9.00%	9.89%	42.00%	72.41%	75.00%	300.00%
10.00%	11.11%	43.00%	75.44%	76.00%	316.67%
11.00%	12.36%	44.00%	78.57%	77.00%	334.78%
12.00%	13.64%	45.00%	81.82%	78.00%	354.55
13.00%	14.94%	46.00%	85.19%	79.00%	376.19%
14.00%	16.28%	47.00%	88.68%	80.oo%	400.00%
15.00%	17.75%	48.00%	92.31%	81.00%	426.32%
16.00%	19.05%	49.00%	96.08%	82.00%	455.56%
17.00%	20.48%	50.00%	100.00%	83.00%	488.24%
18.00%	21.95%	51.00%	104.08%	84.00%	525.00%
19.00%	23.46%	52.00%	108.33%	85.00%	566.67%
20.00%	25.00%	53.00%	112.77%	86.00%	614.29%
21.00%	26.58%	54.00%	117.39%	87.00%	669.23%
22.00%	28.21%	55.00%	122.22%	88.00%	733.33%
23.00%	29.87%	56.00%	125.27%	89.00%	809.09%
24.00%	31.48%	57.00%	132.56%	90.00%	900.00%
25.00%	33.33%	58.00%	138.10%	91.00%	1011.11%
26.00%	35.14%	59.00%	143.90%	92.00%	1150.00%
27.00%	36.99%	60.00%	150.00%	93.00%	1328.57%
28.00%	38.89%	61.00%	156.41%	94.00%	1566.67%
29.00%	40.95%	62.00%	143.16%	95.00%	1900.00%
30.00%	42.86%	63.00%	170.27%	96.00%	2400.00%
31.00%	44.93%	64.00%	177.78%	97.00%	3233.33%
32.00%	47.06%	65.00%	185.71%	98.00%	4900.00%
33.00%	49.25%	66.00%	194.12%	99.00%	9900.00%
				100.00%	

Fig. 6.10

achieving your break-even profit point, then you would have to mark your goods up by:

$$\text{Profit markup} = \frac{20 \text{ (profit)}}{100 \text{ (price)} - 20 \text{ (profit}} \times 100$$

$$= \frac{20 \text{ (profit)}}{80 \text{ (cost)}} \times 100$$

$$= 25\%$$

To help you check your calculations, refer to the conversion chart in Fig. 6.10.

The final step is to apply this markup to a range of jobs or products to check whether it will result in competitive prices.

The projected profit and loss account

Having detailed and classified all of your costs, decided on a selling price(s) and arrived at a break-even profit point to give you the necessary sales volume to achieve your net profit goal, you are ready to compile a summary of the

	£	£
Sales:		100 000
Stock costs (net of closing stock):	75 000	
Gross profit:		25 000
Overheads		
Rent:	4 000	
Utilities:	2 000	
Advertising:	3 000	
Professional fees:	1 500	
General expenses:	1 500	
	12 000	
Net profit before tax:		13 000

Fig. 6.11 Projecting and compiling a profit and loss account

expected profit position of your business at the end of its first year's trading. This summary is known as a profit and loss account. In its simplest form it shows the expected sales revenue and details of total costs which have been incurred within the trading year. The costs are subtracted from the sales revenue to give the gross and net profits. It is laid out as shown in the example given in Fig. 6.11.

The *sales revenue* is taken directly from the BEPP. If your BEPP is physical units of production, then obviously sales volume will have to be multiplied by selling price to obtain sales revenue.

The *cost of stock sold* is the variable cost in this case. If variable costs have been plotted on a break-even chart, the figure is simply read off the chart. If a percentage margin has been used to arrive at BEPP, then the percentage of sales revenue that is variable cost will be 100 (sales revenue or selling price) minus the profit margin. For example, if the profit margin is 25% then the cost of goods must be 75% of the sales revenue.

The *fixed costs* are simply entered from your estimates.

Summary

Detailing and classifying the costs of your business and examining the way in which they interact with sales volume and selling price is the key to establishing the profit or loss it may make. It is a major part of the planning process for any new business venture and should be carried out with as much accuracy as possible. Once completed, it should be referred to constantly as the business grows; comparison of projected and actual costs should be monitored closely and acted on as necessary.

The results of your costing exercise may require you to carry out further market research or to even revise the nature of your business venture. Do not become disheartened by this for the costing will have served its purpose in preventing you from making costly if not ruinous mistakes

If the conclusion of your work with this chapter is that your business venture will make a profit, do not automatically assume the business is viable, for you might not be able to finance its overall capital requirements.

Checklist

---

1. Do you know the difference between cost and capital?
2. Have you made a full assessment of all of your fixed costs including:
   - depreciation
   - interest charges
   - administration
   - production
   - selling (including advertising budget)
   - maintenance and repairs
   - utilities: telephone, electricity, gas and water
   - transport
   - miscellaneous budget
   - full cost of permanent staff
   - professional fees (accountant/solicitor)?
3. Can any of your fixed costs be reduced by:
   - delaying purchases
   - buying second-hand?
4. Are all of your fixed costs necessary?
5. Have you compared the cost of leasing fixed assets to outright purchase?
6. Have you made a full assessment of your variable costs?
7. Have you fully researched suppliers of stock, equipment and services?
8. Have you chosen your suppliers of stock, equipment and services on some objective basis as:
   - delivery times
   - price
   - discount terms on bulk purchases
   - delivery cost
   - payment terms
   - quality and reliability?
9. How will the work be organized?
10. Can you reduce your variable costs by better organizing production, selling or administration?
11. Have you estimated your target profit?
12. Does it allow for a satisfactory rate of return on the capital employed in your business?
13. Does it allow for retaining profits in the business to finance future trading?

14. What is your break-even sales figure, best and worst estimate?
15. What is your break-even profit sales figure, best and worst estimate?
16. Does your market research information confirm that your break-even figures are achievable?
17. What margin of safety have you allowed?
18. Are your costings too optimistic?
19. If necessary, have you selected and used an appropriate method for compiling job estimates?
20. Do you know the difference between a percentage margin and a percentage markup?
21. Have you compiled a projected profit and loss account to show the expected position at the end of your first year's trading?

7

how much capital will you need?

What fixed assets will your business need? • How much working capital will your business need? • How much cash will your business need? • Summary • Checklist • Answer to cashflow forecast and balance sheet problem

One of the most common mistakes made by potential new businesses is getting wrong the total money/capital requirements for efficiently starting up and operating their new venture – you can't afford to make such a mistake.

The actual amount you need will of course vary with the scale and nature of your business, but all businesses will have to find capital for two specific purposes:

● The acquisition of items which the business expects to keep for a long period of time (i.e. for periods greater than a year) such as premises and equipment – these are known as *fixed assets* and accordingly the capital necessary to acquire them is known as *fixed capital*.
● The provision of sufficient monies to operate the business on a day-to-day basis. This is known as *working capital* and is needed to cover payments for such items as stock, materials and wages which have to be paid for on a regular basis throughout the trading year. This capital is constantly 'working' to keep the business alive.

Together, the capital requirements in each of these areas will represent the total amount of money you will need to invest in the business at any one time. The best way forward is to examine each broad area of capital requirements in turn.

What fixed assets will your business need?

Nearly all businesses will require a certain amount of fixed capital. For many the acquisition of premises will represent the largest fixed capital investment they will make, and partly for this reason this is dealt with in a chapter of its own. For some small service businesses operating from home (e.g. mobile hairdressing) fixed capital expenditure could be low, consisting perhaps of a few items of inexpensive equipment and a second-hand car. Different businesses will require different fixed assets to make the manufacture or provision of their end product or service possible. An example of a possible fixed asset requirement schedule for a small retail business is given in Fig. 7.1.

	Investments (£)
Premises (leasehold, 2000 sq. ft.):	18 000
Shop frontage sign and decor:	2 500
Display stands and shelving:	3 000
Freezer display units:	1 750
Chiller display units:	1 750
Cold storage:	1 000
Pricing guns (2):	120
Trolleys and baskets:	300
Miscellaneous equipment:	200
Electronic till:	700
Micro computer (accounts/stock control):	1 200
Small delivery van:	7 500
	38 020

Fig. 7.1 Fixed assets for a small food store

A number of factors will influence your decisions as to what items you should acquire and on what scale. These can be roughly listed under the following headings:

● The market for your business – you will have to acquire assets that are consistent in their attributes with the needs of your customers.
● The nature of your product/service – obviously, each product and service will need different assets to make its manufacture/ selling and distribution to customers possible.
● The goals of your business – your 'shopping list' for fixed assets must be consistent with what you intend your business to achieve in terms of its markets, profitability and organization. It is certainly a good idea to list your business's goals along with their separate resource/asset requirements. For example, the goal: reducing shop-lifting to 2% of sales

would require an effective surveillance and security system, possibly implying the necessity of such assets as closed-circuit TV surveillance and security mirrors.
● The scale of finance at your disposal – most small businesses have limited finance available with which to purchase assets. In effect, there will be competition between various investment proposals for this limited finance. In deciding whether or not to acquire any fixed asset you should ask yourself the following questions:
● What will it do for my business?
● Is it really needed?
● Will the acquisition of the asset prevent the business from acquiring other assets? If so, what effect would that have on the business?
● Is there an alternative item available that will achieve similar ends? If so, which will represent the most cost-effective purchase?

➤ *Carefully consider the effect these factors will have on your requirements and compile your fixed asset list.*

How much working capital will your business need?

The circulation of working capital

We have seen that fixed capital will stay 'locked up' in fixed assets for a long time. Working capital is more 'liquid' in that it changes its form more rapidly. To illustrate this, look at the way working capital circulates in a small manufacturing business, McKenzie Limited, shown in Fig. 7.2. Money goes out to buy materials, services and labour needed to produce and sell the finished product, and eventually money comes back as customers pay cash. Following the cycle through, working capital changes from money into raw materials, then into partly finished goods (inclusive of the conversion costs: rates, wages, electricity, etc.), then into stocks of finished products, then into 30-day loans made to customers who have bought the products under such payment terms, and then finally back into cash as the customers settle their accounts. In our example, on any given day there will be money in the bank (or there should be if the business is to remain solvent!) to meet payments for supplies, wages and

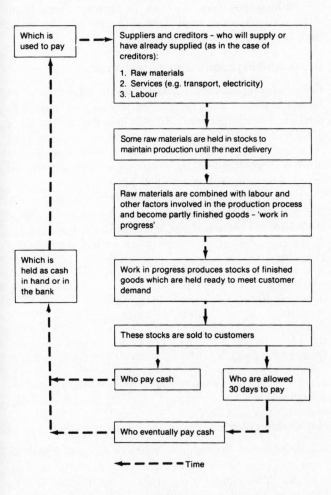

Fig. 7.2 The flow of working capital

other expenses, stocks of raw materials, work in progress and finished products, cash coming in from sales and money owing to the business from customers who have not yet settled their accounts. All these items represent things that the business possesses, they are its current assets. Being differentiated from its fixed assets in that they will be turned back into cash (hopefully!) in the near future.

Gross working capital and current assets

For an existing business, if you add up the total value of its current assets on any one day you will have calculated its total gross working capital. To illustrate, the calculation of McKenzie Limited's gross working capital on 3 August 1988 is shown in Fig. 7.3. However, what is very important to note is that that is the total gross working capital requirements for 3 August 1988 and that more working capital may be required a day, a week or a month later. For instance, if McKenzie Limited plan to increase sales, then it is obvious that more working capital will have to be invested in the full range of its current assets to make those sales possible.

	£	
Cash in hand:	1500	(ready to pay suppliers
Raw materials:	3000	& expenses)
Work in progress:	2500	
Finished products:	1500	
Debtors	700	(total value of customer accounts
Gross working capital	9200	outstanding on 3 August 1988)

Fig. 7.3 Total gross working capital on McKenzie Limited on 3 August 1988

Net working capital

In case you were beginning to worry that you will have to fund all the gross working capital requirements of your business, take a sigh of relief, as that is not the case. Just as businesses have things that they possess, assets, they also have things that they owe, liabilities. Short-term liabilities such as trade credit and overdrafts, known as *current liabilities*, reduce the working capital that has to be found from the internal resources of the business (or, if you prefer the term, 'from your own pocket'). The difference between current assets and current liabilities is the amount your business will have to contribute to gross working capital: it is known as *net working capital*.

Obtaining interest-free trade credit (usually 30 days) is the best method of reducing net working capital requirements. For example, imagine a business with no current asset requirements other than stock, that can obtain 30-day credit from its supplier and sell all that stock within 28 days of receipt: it would have net working capital requirements of nil In effect, the supplier of the goods would be funding all the gross working capital requirements for free! However, in reality this is rarely the case. A business operating in such a way may in fact expose itself to severe cash flow problems if it fails to turn its stock into cash in sufficient time to meet the payment deadline (see 'cash flows' on p. 152).

Calculating your working capital requirements

The working capital your business will require at any one time is dependent on:

● The length of time it will take for the working capital to complete the cycle from cash to stocks and back into cash again; and
● The level of sales it has to support.

The longer it takes to complete the cycle and the higher your level of sales, the more gross working capital you will need to run the business.

Let us examine the commonest current assets you might have to fund, stock and debtors, including how to establish/calculate their individual working capital requirements. The other major current asset all businesses require is cash – this will warrant lengthy discussion and will be dealt with separately.

Stock

If you hold stocks of finished goods or raw materials you will have to solve the problem of how big those stocks will have to be. The two main factors which will affect the size of your stocks are as follows:

● The usage rate – the daily, weekly or monthly rate at

which finished goods are sold or raw materials consumed by the production process.

● The lead time between placing an order and receiving the goods or the time lapse between deliveries.

The weekly time lapse between deliveries multiplied by the weekly usage rate plus a margin of safety will determine the necessary maximum stock level to maintain the business. The smaller the time lapse between deliveries, the smaller the working capital that is required for stock. The example in Fig. 7.4. clearly shows this relationship.

When stocks are at a maximum just after delivery, XYZ enjoys the benefit of operating with £4000 less working capital than ABC due to the simple fact that it has secured more frequent supplies. Effectively this means that XYZ has a faster cycle of working capital. ABC has to wait four weeks to realize the full return on the capital it has invested whereas XYZ only has to wait two weeks.

It is impossible to make any general rules about the minimum stock levels you must hold – each business will have its own peculiarities. Suffice it to say that when compiling an estimate you should carefully assess customer demand. For instance, what breadth and depth of stocks will they demand you to have on hand or display? The greater your stock range, the greater your minimum stock level will have to be.

An alternative or complementary way to estimate your average stock requirements is to refer to the average rate of stock-turn for your type and size of business in published statistics. The rate of stock-turn figure is the number of times the average holding of stock has been sold in a given period

	ABC Ltd	*XYZ Ltd*
Weekly sales @ cost (i.e. usage rate of stock):	£2000	£2000
Lead time in weeks:	4 ×	2 ×
Value of reorder to maintain stocks:	£8000	£4000
	+	+
Minimum safety stocks held:	£1000	£1000
Maximum stock level:	£9000	£5000

Fig. 7.4 The effect of different lead times on stock level

$$\text{Rate of stock-turn} = \frac{\text{Value of the volume of sales for the period}}{\text{Value of average stock level}}$$

(**Note:** both sales and stock should be at the same valuation. For example, if the stock level is valued at cost price so must the sales volume.)

Fig. 7.5 Calculation of rate of stock-turn

of time (usually one year). It is obtained by the simple formula shown in Fig. 7.5.

The rate of stock-turn (RST) is in effect a measure of how long stocks are held for and consequently the circulation speed of working capital in the business – the more frequently stock is turned over (bought and sold), the less working capital is required to finance stocks. An RST of 52 per annum means that one week's stock is on hand; an RST of 12 per annum means that one month's stock is held, and so on.

If you know what rate of stock-turn you can reasonably expect for your type and scale of business and your estimated sales for your first year's trading (from market research, Chapter 3) then it is a relatively easy matter to calculate/estimate the amount of working capital you will have tied up in stocks and for how long. For instance, if you were planning to open a newsagents with an estimated RST of 5.6 and projected sales of £120 000 per annum, then you could reasonably expect that:

● On average you will have to hold 65 days' worth of stock, because stock is expected to be turned over 5.6 times in the year – 365/5.6 = 65.
● The retail value of that stock will be £21 370 – (65/365) × £120 000 = £21 370 (on average).
● If the margin of profit on that stock is 36%, then the valuation at cost will be £13 677, because 100% = retail value, 36% = profit, cost = 100% – 36%, therefore 64% of £21 370 (64/100 21 370) = £13 677.

The method to estimate how much working capital (on average) you will have tied up in stock is simplified in Fig. 7.6. The method to calculate a day's stock is simplified in Fig. 7.7.

Average stock level $=\dfrac{\text{Value of the volume of sales for period}}{\text{Rate of stock-turn}}$

Note: If you use a sales estimate valued at selling price then the value of average stock you obtain will also be at selling price. Thus, to revalue the stock at cost price (i.e. what you will pay for it), you have to reduce its value by your expected gross profit percentage margin. (For a full discussion of gross profit and the calculation of percentage margins, see Chapter 6.)

Fig. 7.6 Calculation of average stock requirements for a given level of sales using annual rate of stock-turn

Day's stock held $=\dfrac{\text{Value average stock level}}{\begin{array}{c}\text{Value of volume of sales}\\\text{per annum}\end{array}} \times 365$ (days in period)

Note: Both sales and stock should be at the same valuation, either cost or selling price. If you want to compare day's stock held to day's credit given by your supplier you should value both sales and stock at cost.

Fig. 7.7 Calculation of days stock held

If you expect to secure trade credit it is useful to compare the number of days' credit given (on average) by your suppliers to the number of days stock is held (on average) to estimate your average net working capital requirements for stock. If the newsagents in the previous example could secure 30-day trade credit then it would effectively reduce the time average stocks are held from 65 to 35 days. The business would only have to finance 35 days' worth of stock instead of 65. Hence, the net working capital required to finance its average stock-holding would decrease from £13 677 to £7 366, i.e. (35/65) £13 677:

Assets:

Stock:	£13 677

Liabilities:

Creditor:	£6 312
Net working capital:	£7 365

> ➤ *Try and find out the information on working capital*
> *requirements for stock from one of the following sources:*
>
> ● Trade magazines, trade associations, government
> statistics, talking to people in your line of business.
> ● Obtain copies of final accounts of businesses for sale,
> similar to the type you intend to set up. The accounts should
> contain the necessary information, sales and stock figures, for
> you to use the formula given in Fig. 7.5 to calculate the
> business's rate of stock-turn. Calculate the RST for a number
> of businesses, take an average and apply it to your venture.

If you are going to be involved in manufacturing or
providing a service which involves 'adding value' to raw
materials, then don't forget your 'stocks' will consist of raw
materials, work in progress (WIP) and finished goods. Raw
materials will be valued at the cost price of their purchase
but WIP and finished goods will have labour and overhead
costs 'stored up' in them (look again at the cycle of working
capital in Fig. 7.2). Consequently, the valuation of WIP and
finished goods stocks must be inclusive of the conversion
costs. To estimate working capital requirements in such a
case will therefore require a detailed breakdown of unit costs
(see Chapter 6) in addition to projecting the average days
held of each category of stocks.

The following example illustrates how to calculate the
working capital requirements for the three types of stock to
achieve a given sales target.

HS Alarms is a new business planning to manufacture and
sell home security systems. In its first year it expects to
achieve sales of 10 000 units. The detailed breakdown of
costs to achieve this level of sales is as follows:

	£
Materials:	50 000
Labour:	20 000
Overheads:	20 000
	90 000
Profit:	10 000
	100 000

HS Alarms have also projected that:

1. They will have to hold raw material stocks representing three weeks' usage (based on a combination of the minimum size of an economic reorder quantity and lead time).
2. WIP will take two weeks to pass through the production process.
3. They will have to hold two weeks' stock of finished security systems to meet their market's need for immediate delivery.

To aid financial planning, HS Alarms will have to calculate the amount of working capital that will be required to fund stocks of raw materials, WIP and finished products. The calculation is shown in Fig. 7.8 and the working capital cycle clearly illustrated in Fig. 7.9.

Raw materials:
Three weeks stock (3/52 x £50 000): 2885

WIP: Two weeks' stock:
    Raw material content (2/52 x £50 000): 1923
    Labour and overhead content ([2/52 x £40 000]/2): 769

(As each stage of the production process is expected to use (absorb) equal proportions of overhead and labour expenses, the value of these expenses used (absorbed) by the WIP is averaged at half the total cost of converting raw materials to finished products.)

Finished products:
    Two weeks' stock (2/52 x £90 000): 3462
    Gross woing capital required: 9038

Fig. 7.8 Projection of HS Alarms' gross working capital requirements

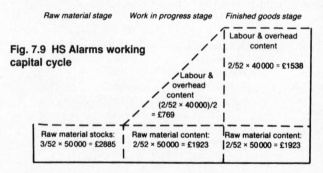

Fig. 7.9 HS Alarms working capital cycle

Raw material stage   Work in progress stage   Finished goods stage

Labour & overhead content
2/52 × 40 000 = £1538

Labour & overhead content
(2/52 × 40 000)/2 = £769

Raw material stocks: 3/52 × 50 000 = £2885 | Raw material content: 2/52 × 50 000 = £1923 | Raw material content: 2/52 × 50 000 = £1923

Debtors

Selling on credit lengthens the working capital cycle and thereby increases the amount of working capital required to operate the business.

For instance, if HS Alarms (in our previous example) was to offer 30 days' settlement terms to all its customers it would increase its gross working capital requirements (on average) by £7397 (30/365 days × £90 000). However, allowing for slow payers the actual length of credit taken would probably be 45 days, an increase of £11 096 (45/365 days × £90 000)!

If you plan to sell on credit, work out the greatest and least demands credit sales will make on working capital. As a general guide to working out the lengths of credit your customers will take, increase the days' credit allowed by at least a half to account for slow payers. If you are going to sell to other businesses find out how fast they usually settle their accounts. You will probably discover that many companies (in particular the larger ones) will think nothing of taking up to three months to pay! Failure now to investigate the days' credit your potential customers may take will probably spell disaster for you in the future.

How much cash will your business need?

Cash, profit and capital

It is not uncommon for newcomers to business to mistake cash for profit. Cash and profit are two distinct terms. Cash can come from a variety of sources: loans, overdrafts, retained profits, etc. Profits come from the difference between a business's revenue and its costs.

If a business is under-capitalized (i.e. not enough finance has been placed in the business for fixed assets and working capital), then part or all of the profits will have to be retained to make up the shortfall. Profits will then be tied up financing such items as equipment, stocks, bills that have to be paid in advance, debtors etc. It can be easily seen that profit is not necessarily in the form of a growing bank balance. Consequently a business can be making a healthy profit but be overdrawn at the bank. This position is fine if it is controlled, planned for and temporary – it is when it becomes uncontrolled, unplanned and permanent that disaster strikes. Cash is the life blood of a business and without it new materials, wages, stock, etc. cannot be purchased.

Cash flows

You should now be fully familiar with the idea that working capital circulates in the business and as it does so changes its form (e.g. cash → stock→ debtors → cash). Cash as part of the cycle flows into and out of the business. For a business to continue trading, there must be more cash coming in (from whatever source) than going out, otherwise it will be unable to meet its liabilities (debts); it will become insolvent. If the owner of such a business continues to trade knowing that such a situation exists, then he or she will be liable to prosecution for fraudulent trading. At the very least, creditors will make claims in law against such a business and these could lead to bankruptcy.

To minimize the risk of insolvency, all businesses should forecast their cash needs. Before you start your business you must prepare what is known as a cash flow forecast for your first year's trading. This is a month-by-month or week-by-week forecast of how much cash will be coming in and how much will be going out. To some extent you probably already do this with your own personal finances but in a less formal way.

'If Bob pays me back that money he owes me on time and I get that tax rebate I should be able to cover the electricity bill at the end of the month ... but how am I going to find enough cash for the holidays the following month ... I wonder if I will get that pay rise?'

To draw up a cash flow forecast you will need to know:
- How much cash is coming in, when and from where.
- How much cash is going out, when and where to.

➤ *But before you attempt to do this for your business idea, compile a cash flow forecast for your own personal or family finances – this will help you understand the process involved.*

Forecasting personal and family cash needs

► First, prepare a list of cash in and cash out, as in the examples in Fig. 7.10 and then use this information to compile a cash flow forecast as in Fig. 7.11.

Cash in:

Item	When received	Comments
David's wages	monthly	£600 net, increases to £650 in September
Sue's wages	weekly	part-time shop worker; gaines extra hours in the summer and Christmas periods

Cash out:

Item	When received	Comments
Mortgage	monthly	£175 per month
Life assurance	monthly	£40 per month
:oan	monthly	£38 per month
Gas	quarterly	use previous years' bills and allow for price increases and extra appliances
Electricity	quarterly	as above
Telephone	quarterly	previous bills show little change over the year
Water rates	half year	£53 in October; £63 in April
House insurance	quarterly	£28 per quarter
TV licence	per annum	£55
Car tax	half year	£55
Car insurance	per annum	£200
Petrol	—	£48 per month
Clothes	—	new clothes for holidays and school clothes children in September
Food	—	£180 per month
Miscellaneous	—	£100 per month – general expenses
Holidays	—	£280
Christmas	—	£200 presents, etc.

Fig. 7.10

153

	July	Aug	Sept	Oct	Nov	Dec
Cash In:						
Wages 1	600	600	650	650	650	650
Wages 2	200	200	100	100	100	320
Total cash in:	800	800	750	750	750	970
Cash out:						
Mortgage:	175	175	175	175	175	175
Life ins:	40	40	40	40	40	40
Credit cards:	28	28	28	28	28	28
Rates:	42	42	42	42	42	42
Bank loan:	38	38	38	38	38	38
Gas:			30			50
Electric:			60			90
Telephone:		47			47	
Water rates:				53		
House ins:		28			28	
TV lic:						
Car tax:				55		
Car ins:				100		
Petrol:	48	48	48	48	48	48
Clothes:		100				100
Food:	180	180	180	180	180	180
Miscellaneous:	40	40	40	40	40	40
Misc:		20	20	20	20	20
Holiday:		280				
Christmas:						300
Total cash out:	591	1066	701	819	686	1151
Monthly balance:	209	(266)	49	(69)	64	(181)
Opening balance:	0	209	(57)	(8)	(77)	(13)
Closing balance: (Cumulative)	209	(57)	(8)	(77)	(13)	(194)

Fig. 7.11

The top of the cash flow forecast shows the cash coming in, in our example David's and Sue's wages; the middle section shows the cash going out each month; and the bottom half shows the all-important monthly cash balances. The first balance shows the surplus (or deficit in brackets) for each month (total cash in minus total cash out); the second is the opening balance for the month (the

Jan	Feb	Mar	April	May	June		Totals:
650	650	650	650	650	650		7 700
80	80	80	80	80	130		1 550
730	730	730	730	730	780		9 250
175	175	175	175	175	175		2 100
40	40	40	40	40	40		480
28	28	28	28	28	28		336
42	42	42	42	42	42		504
38	38	38	38	38	38		456
		50			40		170
		90			60		300
	47			47			188
			63				116
	28			28			112
55							55
			55				110
							100
48	48	48	48	48	48		576
							200
180	180	180	180	180	180		2 160
40	40	40	40	40	40		480
20	20	20	20	20	20		220
							280
							300
666	686	751	729	686	711		9 243
64	44	(21)	1	44	69		7
(194)	(130)	(86)	(107)	(106)	(62)		
(130)	(86)	(107)	(106)	(62)	7		

closing balance from the previous month brought forward);
and the third is the closing balance (the cumulative cash
position, calculated by adding the monthly cash surplus or
deficit to the opening balance for the month).

David's and Sue's cash flow forecast shows that they will
need to obtain an overdraft from the bank for the greater
part of the year, or attempt to reduce expenditure on some
items if possible. The main cause of their shortage of cash is
the planned expenditure on a holiday in August. As their

155

total cash flows in only exceed total cash flows out by £7 over the course of the year, it would be perhaps wise for them to forgo the holiday this year. Whatever they decide, they now have useful information and a good method at their disposal to look into the future, know when problems are on the way and be able to take action to prevent them.

Forecasting cash needs for a business start-up

Compiling a cash flow forecast for a new business is similar to the exercise you have just carried out for your personal or family cash needs. The difference will be in where the cash comes from and where it goes to. There will also be a greater degree of difficulty in estimating the timing and volume of the cash inflows and outflows. Let's look at cash in and cash out in turn and then consider a fully worked example.

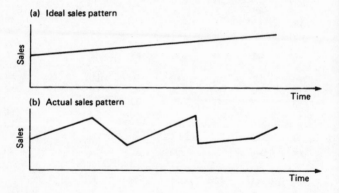

Fig. 7.12

Cash in

Cash coming into a business comes from a number of sources: sales, owner's capital and loan capital.

Sales

Ideally any business person would like to see his/her sales evenly spread out over the year (as in Fig. 7.12(a)). Clearly this would make the business easier to plan and operate.

However, depending on the nature of the market for your business (see Chapter 3) your sales pattern will probably look more like that shown in Fig. 7.12(b).

The first task then is to translate your sales pattern into an estimate of monthly sales. How you do this will depend on the nature of the information gained from your market research and its detail.

If all of your sales are on a cash basis, then the pattern of your cash inflows will be the same as your sales pattern. However, if your business will sell all or part of its products/services on a credit basis, then the cash from those sales will lag behind the actual sales by the average days' credit taken by your customers. For example, if you are offering one month's settlement terms then the cash from sales made in January will not come in until February, perhaps even later when you account for slow payers (as noted earlier in the chapter).

How accurate your sales projections will be depends on the number and nature of assumptions you have to make. Obviously, nobody can predict the future with 100% accuracy so therefore the golden rule in compiling a cash flow projection is to:

● underestimate cash coming in from sales; and
● overestimate cash going out

It is better to be pleasantly surprised by having more cash than expected rather than having to face an unexpected cash crisis six months after you have started.

Capital

To start the business it is obvious that a certain amount of money is required to be put in to finance a variety of purchases so that sales can be generated. There will be injections of capital. It will either come from your own personal funds or from long- or short-term loans (see Chapter 8). You can obtain an approximation of the amount of capital you will have to find by adding together your estimates of fixed and average working capital requirements for your first year. However, this will not be entirely accurate because it will not take into account or include:

● variations in working capital requirements associated

with fluctuating sales over time
- the timing of your fixed asset purchases
- the size and timings of your own personal drawings from the business

You can, of course, calculate your exact working capital requirements for each monthly or weekly period. However, this can prove rather tedious. The compilation of the cash flow will help you to decide the actual size, timing and nature of the capital injections you will have to put into the business. A simple method is to draw up a 'first' cash flow forecast without any capital input, then substitute different scales and timings of capital injections until a satisfactory cumulative cash flow position is reached. As this indicates the cash flow forecast, it is an ideal tool for solving 'if, what' type problems, e.g.'If I increase the initial capital input by £2000, what effect will that have on my cumulative cash flow in month four?'

Cash out

Cash outflows will result from expenditure on

- Fixed costs (overheads), e.g. rent, rates, electricity, etc.
- Variable or direct costs – for most this will be mainly stock.
- Fixed asset purchases, e.g. premises and equipment.
- Personal drawings.
- Loan repayments (net of interest).
- Taxation payments.

Overheads

These are the easiest to predict because by definition they are not affected by short-term fluctuations in sales (see Chapter 6). You will have to research in detail the timing of such payments. Here is a rough guide.

- Utilities such as electricity and gas are paid quarterly in arrears. However, it is possible you may have to pay connection charges or a deposit if you are a new customer. If you wish to spread the costs more evenly over time you can have your future bills estimated and arrange for monthly payments to be made direct from your bank account.
- Rent is usually paid in advance. The terms of leases vary but it is not uncommon to pay quarterly or six-monthly in advance.

● Buildings and contents insurance is usually paid for in advance. However, most insurance companies will usually arrange monthly payments.

● Wages/salaries are usually paid a week or a month in arrears. It is obviously better to pay monthly than weekly as this shortens the net working capital cycle. PAYE and NI deductions from wages will be paid monthly in arrears. Therefore, net wages (i.e. after deductions) should be shown separately on the cash flow forecast.

● Advertising budget – if you intend to promote your business effectively you will have to compile a sales promotion plan (Chapter 4 tells you how to do it). Such a plan should also contain the size and timing of the costs involved.

● Motor vehicle expenses – road tax and insurance can be readily estimated; petrol with a little more difficulty. The main problem is with unexpected expenditure on such items as repairs, etc. One way to account for the unexpected is to allocate a sum to a contingency fund for such eventualities. Another is to lease the vehicle (the lease to cover repairs, etc.) or to take out a maintenance contract which includes regular servicing and breakdowns – this is equally applicable to other forms of equipment and machinery.

● Professional fees – expenditure on legal and accountancy services will undoubtedly be erratic. You will perhaps make more use of such services in the initial start-up and at the end of your trading year as your final accounts are drawn up.

● Miscellaneous items – this will include expenditure on numerous minor items such as coffee, stationery, cleaning materials, etc. For cash flow purposes it is better to put the same amount down each month.

Variable costs

These, by definition, will vary with sales. Therefore in the first instance, the accuracy of predicted cash outflows related to variable costs will directly depend on the accuracy of monthly sales estimates. For many businesses the largest single item representing continuous cash outflows is stock purchase. Much has already been said about stocks; detailed consideration must also be given to:

● the size of initial stock
● the frequency at which stocks will be replaced
● the payment terms

Initial stocks. Calculating the size of the initial stock level can prove a problem. For a retail business the simplest method is to use the annual rate of stock-turn (as discussed earlier). For example, if the expected rate of stock-turn is 12 and the projected sales are £120 000, then the initial stocks will be £10 000 at retail prices. However, this method neglects the fact that sales will vary from month to month and will probably be well below the norm in the first few months of trading, resulting in too much stock being carried when sales are low. A refinement is to apply the RST per annum as a ratio of stock to sales for the sales pattern over a shorter term, say two or three months. For example, a business with expected RST of 12 per annum and sales of £18 000 for the first quarter would require initial stocks of £6000. Neither method is perfect so you may quite legitimately choose a compromise between the two or some alternative method based on detailed knowledge of the stock requirements of your particular business.

Frequency of deliveries. The more often a business can obtain deliveries, the fewer days, weeks or months in advance it has to buy stock. A business that only receives deliveries every two months faces the situation of having stock to sell in March delivered in January. In times of rapid expansion this can cause severe cash flow problems as stocks have to be built up rapidly from relatively low cash inflows.

Payment terms. If a business has to pay cash on delivery, then purchases in any one month will have to be paid for in that month. However, if a business can secure, for example, one month's credit, then January's purchases will not show on the cash flow forecast until February, February's until March, and so on. Therefore, the impact of poor delivery frequencies on the cash flow can be lessened by securing trade credit.

Capital expenditure

For your major purchases (fixed assets) you must draw up a detailed schedule of amounts and timings of payments. This is simple to do and like most people you will probably find that most of this expenditure will occur in the pre-start-up period of the business.

Personal drawings

This has nothing to do with profits but quite simply the amount you will draw from the business to finance your personal needs. The best way to estimate this is to draw up your own personal cash flow forecast as suggested earlier.

Loan repayments

Like most businesses you will have to borrow money and consequently there will be loan repayments. These will include both capital and interest repayments. As far as the profit and loss account is concerned, the interest will be charged as a cost and the capital repayments will come out of profits, but for the cash flow forecast no distinction need be made. Remember the cash flow forecast is only concerned with cash in and out.

Note: You may not know exactly how much you will need to borrow until you have compiled your first cash flow projection. You can make the necessary adjustments later.

Overdraft interest and bank charges

You will not know the size of the overdraft you will require until you have completed your first cash flow. Let the bank do the calculations for you and then make the necessary adjustments to the cash flow forecast.

Taxation

Depending on the nature and scale of your business, you may pay taxes to the Inland Revenue, National Insurance (NI) contributions (for your employees and yourself) and value added tax (VAT). Similar taxes to VAT are found in the USA, such as sales and inventory taxes, which vary from state to state and county to county. American readers are well advised to contact their local tax collector's office for full information on such taxes in their locality and then carefully examine the effect(s) they may have on cash flow.

Fortunately, taxes on profits will not have to be paid until after year one. However, self-employed National Insurance contributions will be normally paid out on a monthly basis. PAYE and NI deductions from employees will also be on a monthly basis but payable to the Inland Revenue one month in arrears.

161

VAT (see Chapter 9) will be paid quarterly in arrears on the difference between the VAT elements of sales and purchases invoiced in each quarter.

Note: There are several schemes offered in the UK by the Customs & Excise to help alleviate the cash flow problems of VAT-registered businesses who make credit sales. Make enquiries at your local VAT office to find out if one of them is suited to your business operation.

A cash flow example

Important note: To make the following example realistic, VAT, PAYE and National Insurance contributions have been included. You should be warned that the regulations appertaining to these 'taxes' may have altered since the time of writing. In particular, regulations governing VAT are complex so you should clarify any doubts you have about it and your business with your local VAT office or accountant. The present rate of VAT is 17.5%. For more information on taxation, consult Chapter 9. Also, assumptions made about the type and scale of costings, although feasible, should not be interpreted as being the norm for this type and scale of business.

Steve has recently been made redundant from the local steel works and has decided to open a car accessory shop with his £17 000 redundancy money. The shop is to be called Pitstop and will commence trading in August 19—. He has carefully researched the market for his business and the costs involved and put together the following information on which he has based his cash flow forecast in Fig. 7.14.

Sales

Figure 7.13 shows the breakdown of Pitstop's sales for the first twelve months.

Pitstop will allow one month's credit to local garages – so cash from August's credit sales will be received in September, cash from September's credit sales in October, and so on.
 All cash in from sales will be shown inclusive of VAT.

Purchases

The business expects to operate on a 30% profit margin. Therefore the cost of stock purchases should be 70% of the selling price.

The business is expected to have annual rate of stock-turn of six (two months' stock will be held on average). Therefore, an opening stock of £12 800 (at retail prices, excluding VAT), £8960 at cost, excluding VAT (i.e. reduced by the 30% gross margin, 70/100 × £12 800), will be required to support the first two months of trading, August and September. Stocks will be repurchased to maintain this ratio of stock to future sales, so that the purchasing budget for July will be based on projected sales for September. August for October, and so on. On this basis the purchasing budget over the course of the year is projected as in Fig. 7.13.

Purchases will be paid for cash on delivery. After month six, one month's credit will be given by suppliers of stock. Therefore, there will be no cash outflows on stock purchases in February.

Overheads

Item	Cost per annum £	Payment basis/Comments for cash flow
Shop rental:	4 000	Quarterly in advance £1 000
Rates:	480	Monthly £480
Telephone:	240	Quarterly in arrears £69 (inc. VAT)
Power:	1 000	Quarterly in arrears (high in winter)
Insurance:	900	Annually in advance
Van lease:	1 200	Plus £180 VAT
		Monthly in advance £115 (inc. VAT)
Petrol	720	Plus £108 VAT £69 per month
Advertising:	3 400	Plus £510 VAT
		August: £690 (inc. VAT) initial promotion); December: £690 (inc. VAT) (Xmas promotion); April: £460 (inc. VAT) (Spring promotion); other periods: £230 (inc. VAT) per month
Accountant:	1 620	Plus £243 VAT £805 (inc. VAT) start-up
Solicitor:		£575 (inc. VAT) year end £161 (inc. VAT) remaining quarters

Starting your business

General expenses	1 200	Plus £180 VAT Budgeted at £115 (inc. VAT) per month
Wages:	4 080	Two permanent part-time shop workers paid weekly. Monthly £280 net of NI & PAYE
	18 840	

Capital expenditure

Purchase of existing business inclusive of lease, fixtures and fittings and goodwill as assets of the business. Exempt from VAT. Total expenditure £6000. Additional capital expenditure:

Item	Cost	Timing	Inc. VAT
Electronic till	£1000	On start-up	£1150
Display equipment	£2000	On start-up	£2300
Storage equipment:	£1000	On start-up	£1150
Sub-total:	£4000	On start-up	£4600
Second till:	£1000	In December	£1150
Total:	£5000		£5750

Total expenditure inclusive of VAT on fixed assets should be £11 750.

VAT

Steve has agreed to submit his VAT return every quarter in arrears. The first return will be due at the beginning of November.

The business will pay VAT (@ 15%) on purchases of stock, certain overhead costs (as noted above) and fixed assets (as noted above) and charge VAT at the same rate on sales. The estimated VAT payable to, or refundable from, the Customs & Excise at the end of each quarter is calculated by subtracting the VAT payable on purchases of stock, services and fixed assets (input tax) from that charged on invoiced sales (output tax). The total sales forecast (Fig. 7.13) is used to calculate the total of output taxes collected or due (in the case of credit sales). The schedule of monthly stock purchases is used to calculate the quarterly input taxes paid or due to be paid (in the case of purchases acquired on credit after February). Note that even though payment for stocks received in February will not be due until March, the delivery will be invoiced in February.

Sales pattern

	Cash sales		Credit sales		Total sales	
	ex. VAT	plus VAT	ex. VAT	plus VAT	ex. VAT	plus VAT
August	4800	5520	1400	1610	6200	7130
September	5000	5750	1600	1840	6600	7590
October	5300	6095	1700	1955	7000	8050
November	5600	6440	1900	2185	7500	8625
December	6800	7820	2400	2760	9200	10580
January	5100	5865	1000	1150	6100	7015
February	5800	6670	1500	1725	7300	8395
March	6200	7130	1800	2070	8000	9200
April	6600	7590	2000	2300	8600	9890
May	6700	7705	2100	2415	8800	10120
June	7000	8050	2400	2760	9400	10810
July	7100	8165	2600	2990	9700	11155
	72000	82800	22400	25760	94400	108560

Purchasing budget

	Total sales ex. VAT	Purchasing budget @ retail ex. VAT	Purchasing budget @ cost ex. VAT	Purchasing budget @ cost VAT inc.
Start-up:		12800	8960	10304
August	6200	7000	4900	5635
September	6600	7500	5250	6037
October	7000	9200	6440	7406
November	7500	6100	4270	4911
December	9200	7300	5110	5876
January	6100	8000	5600	6440
February	7300	8600	6020	6923
March	8000	8800	6160	7084
April	8600	9400	6580	7567
May	8800	9700	6790	7809
June	9400	10000	7000	8050
July	9700	10500	7350	8452
	94400	114900	80430	92494
Year two:				
August	10000	?	?	?
September	10500	?	?	?

Figures rounded to nearest pound

Fig. 7.13 Pitstop's sales pattern and purchasing budget

	Aug	Sept	Oct	Nov	Dec	Ja
Cash in:						
Capital:	17000					
VAT refunds:				1864		
Cash sales:	5520	5750	6095	6440	7820	5865
Credit sales:		1610	1840	1955	2185	2760
	22520	7360	7935	10259	10005	8625
Cash out:						
Opening stock:	10304					
Stock:	5635	6037	7406	4911	5876	6440
Rent:	1000			1000		
Rates:	40	40	40	40	40	40
Telephone:				69		
Gas & electric:				200		
Insurance:	900					
Van lease:	115	115	115	115	115	115
Petrol:	69	69	69	69	69	69
Advertising:	690	230	230	230	690	230
Acc./solicitor:	805		161			161
General:	115	115	115	115	115	115
Wages:	280	280	280	280	280	280
NI/PAYE:		60	60	60	60	60
Class 2/NI:	18	18	18	18	18	18
Capital exp.:	10600				1150	
Overdraft chg:						
VAT payments:						
Personal:	500	500	500	500	500	500
Total cash out:	31071	7464	8994	7607	8913	8028
Monthly balance:	(8551)	(104)	(1059)	2652	1092	597
Opening balance:		(8551)	(8655)	(9714)	(7062)	(5970)
Closing balance: (Cumulative balance)	(8551)	(8655)	(9714)	(7062)	(5970)	(5373)

Fig. 7.14 Pitstop's cash flow forecast

Feb	Mar	April	May	June	July	Totals:
						17000
						1864
6670	7130	7590	7705	8050	8165	82800
1150	1725	2070	2300	2415	2760	22770
7820	8855	9660	10005	10465	10925	124434
						10304
	6923	7084	7567	7809	8050	73738
1000			1000			4000
40	40	40	40	40	40	480
69			69			207
350			300			850
						900
115	115	115	115	115	115	1380
69	69	69	69	69	69	828
230	230	460	230	230	230	3910
		161			575	1863
115	115	115	115	115	115	1380
280	280	280	280	280	280	3360
60	60	60	60	60	60	660
18	18	18	18	18	18	216
						11750
						-
726			504			1230
500	500	500	500	500	500	6000
3572	8350	8902	10867	9236	10052	123056
4248	505	758	(862)	1229	873	1378
(5373)	(1125)	(620)	138	(724)	505	
(1125)	(620)	138	(724)	505	1378	

Calculation of VAT figures

Quarter August to October inclusive:
Output – tax payable on sales:

Total sales excluding VAT: £19 800, therefore
Total VAT payable on sales (i.e. $15/100 \times$ £19 800)   £2970
                                                            Total A: £2970

Less
Input – tax refundable:

Stock purchases:

Total purchases excluding VAT: £25 550, therefore
Total VAT refundable on stock purchases
(i.e. $15/100 \times$ £25 550):   £3832

Capital expenditure:

Total expenditure on VAT-rated fixed assets: £4600, therefore
Total VAT refundable ($15/115 \times$ £4600):   £600

Overhead expenditure:

Total expenditure (invoiced) on VAT-rated overheads:

Van lease:	345
Petrol:	207
Advertising:	1150
Professional fees:	966
Telephone:	69 *
General:	345
Total:	3082

VAT element refundable ($15/115 \times$ £3082):   £402
                                                            Total B: £4834

*Note: Even though the telephone bill will not be paid until November it is included in the VAT calculations for the first quarter because the date of the invoice (the tax point) will fall in October.

Net VAT payable (A – B) = (£1864). You can see that for the first quarter the Customs & Excise will actually owe Steve quite a sum of money because Pitstop will have paid more VAT than it will have collected (due to the major purchases of fixed assets and opening stock). Steve will receive the money in November.

Quarter November to January inclusive:

Output tax:

Total sales excluding VAT: £22 800
Total VAT payable on sales (i.e. 15/100 × £22 800):   <u>£3420</u>
                                            Total A: <u>£3420</u>

Input tax:

Stock:

Total purchases excluding VAT: £14 980
Total VAT refundable on purchases (i.e. 15/100 × £14 980):   £2247

Capital expenditure:

Total expenditure on fixed assets excluding VAT: £1000
Total VAT refundable (15/100 × £1000):   £150

Overhead expenditure:

Total expenditure (invoiced) on VAT-rated overheads:

Van lease:	345
Petrol:	207
Advertising:	1150
Professional fees:	161
Telephone:	69
General:	345
Total:	2277

VAT element refundable (15/115 × £2277):   <u>£297</u>
                                      Total B: <u>£2694</u>

Net VAT payable (A -- B) = £726

Quarter February to April inclusive:

Output tax:
Total sales excluding VAT: £23 900
Total VAT payable on sales: Total A: £3585

Input tax:

Stock:

Total purchases excluding VAT: £18 760
Total VAT refundable on purchases: £2814

Overhead expenditure:

Total expenditure (invoiced) on VAT-rated overheads:

| Van lease: | 345 |
| Petrol: | 207 |

(continued overleaf)

Starting your business

Advertising:	920
Professional fees:	161
Telephone:	69
General:	345
Total:	2047

VAT element refundable (15/115 × £2047): £267

Total B: £3081

Net VAT payable (A – B) = £504

Quarter May to July inclusive:

Output tax:

Total sales excluding VAT: £27,900
Total VAT payable on sales: Total A: £4185

Input tax:

Stock:

Total purchases excluding VAT: £21 140
Total VAT refundable on purchases: £3171

Overhead expenditure:

Total expenditure (invoiced) on VAT-rated overheads:

Van lease:	345
Petrol:	207
Advertising:	690
Professional fees:	575
Telephone:	69
General:	345
Total:	2231

VAT element refundable (15/115 × £2231): £291

Total B: £3462

Net VAT payable (A – B) = £723
(payable in August of second trading year)

Total output taxes: £14 160
Total input taxes: £14 071

Net VAT payable: £89

Projected profit and loss account

(Net of depreciation and finance charges)

Sales: 94 400

Purchases:	80 430	
Less Planned closing stock:	14 350	
Cost of sales:		66 080
Gross profit (i.e. profits before overhead costs)	28 320	
Less Overheads:	18 840	
Net profit before taxes:		9 480

Personal drawings

Steve has decided to draw £500 from the business each month to cover his personal needs.

Payment of National Insurance and PAYE

Steve will not pay any taxes on the profits of the business until after year one. However, he will have to pay:

(a) To the Inland Revenue's tax office monthly (in arrears) the National Insurance contributions and tax deducted from the 'wage packets' of his two part-time shop workers plus employers' NI contributions. Steve has estimated these at £60 per month.
(b) His own class 2 National Insurance contributions of approximately £18 per calendar month.

An examination of Pitstop's completed cash flow forecast reveals:

1. For the first seven months, Pitstop will not have enough cash to meet its needs. This is because the initial capital injection of £17 000 is not sufficient to cover both capital and working capital requirements.
2. The cash deficit is severe for the first three months. An overdraft facility of some £10 000 will be required, until the VAT refund on fixed assets and stock purchases is received in November.
3. From November, monthly cash surpluses steadily reduce the cash deficit until a positive cash flow position is reached in April. A minor cumulative cash deficit of £724 is the result of the grouping of quarterly bills and is overcome in the following month.
4. Predictably, the one month's delay in paying for stock purchases from February gives a boost to Pitstop's

cumulative cash flow position (by reducing net working capital requirements) from that date onwards. In fact, it can be easily seen that if Pitstop fails to secure one month's credit by February or March at the latest a positive cumulative cash flow position would not be reached by the end of the year. So if Steve could not introduce more capital from other sources, modify expenditure or reduce credit sales and increase cash sales the business would prove an unviable proposition even though it would be making healthy profits.

Where are Pitstop's profits? – the balance sheet

The relationship between Pitstop's expected net profit of £9480 and its cash in hand of £1378 at the end of the year might not be readily obvious. You are probably curious about the whereabouts of two items: the original £17 000 capital and the £9480 net profit. The answer is simply that some of the profits will have been drawn out of the business by Steve and some will have been retained and used, along with all of the original capital, to fund the purchase of fixed assets and net working capital requirements. Let's look at the picture in more detail.

Over the course of the year Steve will have drawn £6216 out of the business to cover his own personal living expenses and National Insurance contributions, leaving £3264 profit in the business. Adding the retained profits to the original capital invested tells us the amount of capital that will be invested in Pitstop at the end of the year: £20 264. As only £1378 is left as cash, the rest must be in other assets.

Let's list them to find out if this is true.

First the major assets (fixed assets) of the business:

Lease of premises:	£6000
Fixtures and fittings:	£5000
	£11 000

Next its current assets:

Cash on hand (from the cash flow):	£1378
Stock: two weeks' stock on hand to finance August and September sales in year 2. Total from the purchasing budget:	£1435

| Debtors: cash from July's credit sales not received yet: | £2990 |
| Makes a total of: | £18 718 |

However, Pitstop has not had to find all of this money. It has financed some of these current assets from outside sources. It owes money to a number of creditors. We must list and subtract all of these short-term liabilities from its current assets to find how much Pitstop has had to use to fund its own working capital.

Current liabilities:

The last delivery of stock has been invoiced but no payment has been made:	£8452
The gas and electric bills should have been received but payment will be delayed until August:	£150
The same with the telephone bill:	£69
A total of £60 has been deducted from July's wage packets but has not yet been paid to the IR:	£60
Finally, Pitstop owe the Customs & Excise a VAT payment for the last quarter of the year:	£723
Making total liabilities of:	£9454
Therefore, Pitstop's net working capital (net current assets) at the end of its first year is (current assets - current liabilities):	£9264

If we now add the fixed assets to the net current assets we will find the total amount of funds that is tied up in the business at the year end

Total assets (net)   £20 264

Which is as we predicted: the total net assets have been financed by Steve's original capital and profits retained in the business.

We have just completed a balance sheet of what Steve's business will look like at the end of his first year of trading. If you take away all the detail, it's not that complicated; it is a list of where the business has obtained its money from (liabilities) and what it has done with it (assets) or, more simply, what it owes and what it has. The two lists are separated into long-term assets and liabilities, and short-term (current) assets and liabilities.

➤ *Try and answer the following questions about Steve's proposed business (the answers are at the end of the chapter):*

Let's look at the worst possible position for Pitstop given the present sales and costs:

(a) if debtors took two months instead of one month to pay up; and

(b) if Pitstop failed to secure one month's credit from its suppliers of stock:

● How much would this increase net working capital requirements by the end of the first year?

● Would the business be viable? If not, why not?

Note: You can answer the question by simply recalculating Pitstop's net working capital for the year end, but for a fuller picture recalculate the cash flow forecast and draw up a new balance sheet.

Summary

You will need to calculate very carefully how much money you need to start and operate the business. The key to the successful management of your resources is in careful scrutiny and planning of your working capital requirements and cycle. A cash flow forecast is essential to any business. Never forget that cash is the life blood of any business. Once forecasts have been made and budgets set, actual performance of the business should be closely monitored and any deviations investigated at once.

If your business idea has passed the tests of these last three chapters you could have a potentially successful business. However, if it hasn't, then don't despair, take it through the cycle again and see if it can be successfully modified. If the situation is worse than that then you can only be pleased that you never ventured any money on the enterprise and all that you have spent is time and effort. Try again!

Checklist

1. What are your business needs?
2. Have you made a fixed asset requirements list?
3. Do you know the amount of capital each will require?
4. Have you considered the alternatives such as buying second-hand, leasing, renting, etc.?
5. Can you delay the purchase of some fixed assets?
6. Are they all really needed?
7. How much stock will you carry on average?
8. How does this compare to other businesses of a similar type?
9. Can you obtain more frequent deliveries?
10. Can you reduce your stock holding by any other methods?
11. What is the length of working capital cycle?
12. Can it be reduced?
13. How much trade credit can you secure?
14. Can you obtain stock on consignment?
15. Can you organize your manufacturing process to reduce WIP?
16. How many days' credit will you give?
17. How many will you take?
18. Have you the necessary information on sales revenue, credit sales, costs and other outgoings to compile a cash flow forecast?
19. Have you produced a cash flow forecast?
20. Have you looked at the best and worst cash positions?
21. Have you relooked at your:
    - working capital cycle
    - fixed asset schedule
    - reassessed your market for increasing cash sales
    - overheads
    - timing of costs
    - to improve your cash position over time?
22. How much of your profits will have to be retained in the business at the year end to finance future expansion?
23. Other?

Answer to cash flow forecast and balance sheet problem

Cashflow forecast

	Aug	Sept	Oct	Nov	Dec	J.
Cash in:						
Capital:	17 000					
VAT refunds:				1 864		
Cash Sales:	5 520	5 750	6 095	6 440	7 820	5 8
Credit Sales:			1 610	1 840	1 955	2 1
	22 520	5 750	7 705	10 144	9 775	8 0
Cash out:						
Opening stock:	10 304					
Stock:	5 635	6 037	7 406	4 911	5 876	6 4
Rent:	1 000			1 000		
Rates:	40	40	40	40	40	4
Telephone:				69		
Gas & electric:				200		
Insurance:	900					
Van lease:	115	115	115	115	115	11
Petrol:	69	69	69	69	69	6
Advertising:	690	230	230	230	690	2
Acc./solicitor:	805		161			1
General:	115	115	115	115	115	11
Wages:	280	280	280	280	280	28
NI/PAYE:		60	60	60	60	6
Class 2/NI:	18	18	18	18	18	1
Capital exp.:	10 600				1 150	
Overdraft chg:						
VAT payments:						
Personal:	500	500	500	500	500	50
Total cash out:	31 071	7 464	8 994	7 607	8 913	8 02
Monthly balance:	(8 551)	(1 714)	(1 289)	2 537	862	2
Opening balance:		(8 551)	(10 265)	(11 554)	(9 017)	(8 15
Closing balance: (Cumulative balance)	(8 551)	(10 265)	(11 554)	(9 017)	(8 155)	(8 13

	Feb	Mar	April	May	June	July		Totals:
								17 000
								1 864
	6 670	7 130	7 590	7 705	8 050	8 165		82 800
	2 760	1 150	1 725	2 070	2 300	2 415		20 010
	9 430	8 280	9 315	9 775	10 350	10 580		121 674
								10 304
	6 923	7 084	7 567	7 809	8 050	8 452		82 190
	1 000			1 000				4 000
	40	40	40	40	40	40		480
	69			69				207
	350			300				850
								900
	115	115	115	115	115	115		1 380
	69	69	69	69	69	69		828
	230	230	460	230	230	230		3 910
			161			575		1 863
	115	115	115	115	115	115		1 380
	280	280	280	280	280	280		3 360
	60	60	60	60	60	60		660
	18	18	18	18	18	18		216
								11 750
								0
	726			504				1 230
	500	500	500	500	500	500		6 000
	10 495	8 511	9 385	11 109	9 477	10 454		131 508
	1 065)	(231)	(70)	(1 334)	873	126		(9 834)
	8 133)	(9 198)	(9 429)	(9 499)	(10 833)	(9 960)		=====
	9 198)	(9 429)	(9 499)	(10 833)	(9 960)	(9 834)		

Pitstop's Balance Sheet at the end of its first year's trading

Fixed assets

Lease of premises		6 000
		5 000
Total (A)		11 000

Current assets

Prepaid bills		
Stock	14 350	
Debtors	5 750	
Cash in hand		
Total (B)	20 100	

Current liabilities

Trade creditors		
Stock		
Electricity	150	
Gas		
Telephone	69	
Bank overdraft	9 834	
VAT provisions	723	
Tax provisions	60	
Total (C)	10 836	
Net current assets or net working capital (B minus C)		9 264
Net assets employed in the business		20 264

Financed by

Owner's capital introduced	17 000	
Profits retained	3 264	
	20 264	

8

raising finance

*How much is needed? • What will the finance be
required for? • Sources and methods of finance •
Grants • Reducing your need to borrow • Presenting
your case • Summary*

How much is needed?

The first step, of course, is to establish the capital required
to start and operate the business. Chapter 7 should have
enabled you to calculate how much will be needed and,
perhaps more importantly, when it will be needed.

What will the finance be required for?

The next step is to itemize what the finance is required for.
This will set you on the right path to identifying the right
kind of finance to secure. In the course of establishing your
fixed and working capital requirements you will, by
implication, have identified the purposes for which they are
required. Figure 8.1 indicates the appropriate methods of
financing for particular purposes while the next section deals
in more detail with the methods and sources available.

Purpose	Method
Short-term finance	
Debtors, stock, raw materials, and	Overdrafts
other general working capital	Creditors
requirements	Factoring
Long-term finance	
Fixed assets, longer-term	Loans (medium/long)
working capital	Hire purchase
requirements	Grants
	Mortgages
	Equity/venture capital

Fig. 8.1 Identifying the right kind of finance – a summary

Sources and methods of finance

Short-term finance

The *overdraft* is perhaps the commonest and simplest form
of finance available. You and your bank agree a limit to
which you can overdraw on your account. You can then use
part or all of that overdraft facility as and when you need it
which makes this form of finance very flexible. In addition
although the interest rate for overdrafts is usually a few
percentage points above bank rate, the fact that you only
take out the 'loan' when you need it can make it cheap to
operate.

Overdrafts are ideal to cover such requirements as
temporary cash flow problems. They should not, however,
be used to cover the purchase of fixed assets or cover long
term working capital requirements. The reasons for this are
that overdrafts have fluctuating interest rates and can be
reduced or even called in by the bank at very short notice
This makes long-term financial planning with this method of
finance extremely difficult. Moreover, it exposes the business
to the real threat of insolvency. Consider the situation below
where a business attempts to finance most of its working
capital requirements with an overdraft facility:

Current assets:

Stock:	£3000
Debtors:	£1000
	£4000

Current liabilities:

Overdraft:	£4000

If the bank called in or reduced the overdraft it might
possibly force the business into bankruptcy as the debtors
and stock could not be so easily or quickly turned into cash
to repay the overdraft on demand.

To stand any chance of securing a business overdraft the
very least you must do is produce a fully justified cash flow
forecast as described in Chapter 7.

Creditors

Securing trade credit from suppliers is, as previously

iscussed in Chapter 7, a good way of reducing your net orking capital requirements and therefore your overall orrowing. The obvious advantage of this method is that it interest-free. However, the problem is that suppliers are luctant to grant such terms to new businesses. Possibly you ill have to trade on a cash-on-delivery basis until you build p a good track record with your suppliers.

actoring

or small businesses with a large proportion of their sales on edit, a major problem is finding the working capital to nance their customers' debt. If debtors do not pay on time, ish flow problems result. One way to alleviate the problem to engage the services of a 'factor'. A factoring service will dvance up to 80% of the value of credit sales as they are ade, you receive the remainder when your customers settle eir accounts. Cost of factoring varies from as little as 1 to % of your sales turnover. The fee is affected by such nsiderations as the volume of sales involved, number and pe of customers.

Besides easing cash flow problems, use of a factoring rvice can alleviate the problem of administration and ntrol of debtors arising from credit sales. All you have to o is send the sales invoices to the factor who then takes over e whole process of collection.

Factoring is more suitable for businesses whose sales are owing rapidly. By using the factor to finance debtors, cash ows into the business become predictable and therefore the xpansion can be more easily managed.

Although there are many attractions in using a factoring rvice, it should be carefully compared with the dvantages/disadvantages and cost of financing and dministering your own credit sales. Because of the costs volved, businesses whose credit sales are below £60 000 er annum seldom opt for this form of financing debtors. It ould also be noted that using a factoring service reduces ur personal contact with customers.

A list of factoring companies operating in the UK can be btained from the Association of British Factors, 12th Floor, loor House, London EC2Y 5HE.

Short-term loans

These are obtainable from banks and finance houses, bu have limited uses. They are less flexible than an overdra and can work out considerably more expensive when the fu amount is not used. However, they are usually easil arranged if the amount required is relatively small.

Medium- and long-term finance

Loans

These are obtainable from banks and other financia institutions and are ideal for the purchase of fixed asset Banks offer a variety of commercial loans repayable in fro one to ten years. Interest rates can be fixed or variable. Yo must shop around to see what is on offer. For instance, som packages contain repayment 'holidays' where you do no make your first repayment until some months after the loa has been advanced, giving your cash flow a boost in the ear period of trading when it is perhaps most needed.

For the larger and longer-term capital loan, the lendir organization will probably require personal guarantees an security. Where the loan is a 'major' advance to be used t finance the main assets of the business, the lendir institution will look carefully at the 'gearing of the business It will want to know how much you are putting into th business. For small businesses, banks may require you to p at least as much into the business as they are. Therefore, yo will find it difficult to raise a loan in this way if you have le than a 50% stake in your own business.

Note: many small businesses prefer dealing with a ban as the business relationship is more personal. If the ban is kept informed of the progress of your business, buil ing mutual trust and respect, it is likely to be mo sympathetic than other more impersonal lenders whe problems occur.

Hire purchase

Buying business equipment on hire purchase is just the sam as buying household goods on hire purchase. The ma advantage of using this method is that it is relatively easy arrange and secure. The main disadvantages are that intere rates are usually considerably higher than other forms finance and any default on the loan may be pursued vigorously by the lender!

Mortgages

This is a form of finance familiar to most people. Commercial and semi-commercial (when the mortgage is used to purchase a part-residential and part-commercial property) mortgages are advanced for the purchase of specific premises. The maximum loan advanced is usually up to 60% of the valuation of the premises, but sometimes up to 90% in the case of semi-commercial mortgages. Interest rates can either be fixed or variable and the period of the loan can be in excess of 20 years.

Note: building societies do not offer mortgages for industrial purposes. For this type of loan you would have to approach such institutions as finance houses and insurance companies.

Equity finance

This is, by definition, the most permanent form of finance, and is where an individual or organization takes a share in your business. The main disadvantage is obvious: you can lose overall control of your business. The advantages are that there are no repayments involved and the launch of a business venture that you could not previously finance becomes possible.

Equity finance for new businesses goes under the name of 'venture' capital. As there are many sources and types of venture capital available, you should obtain specialist help. Details on venture capital organizations can be obtained from the British Venture Capital Association, 1 Surrey Street, London WC2N 2PS. Tel.: 0171 286 5702.

Grants

I am sure everybody would love to start their business with 'free money'. There are many types of grants available from nearly as many different institutions and organizations, ranging from charities to local and central government bodies. It would take nearly the rest of this book just to go into the sources and types of funds involved.

The availability of grants and criteria for acceptance of

applicants are dependent or based on some or all of the following factors:

1. The area in which you intend to set up your business is an important factor. Most governments are keen to rejuvenate rundown localities such as inner-city areas and under-populated rural areas, particularly those that are suffering from a net migration of population.
2. With a general increase in unemployment your business is more likely to be eligible for a grant if it is going to create employment.
3. Many grants and schemes are related to quite specific business activities. You would be well advised to try and identify the national/local private or public body department representing your type of business activity and check on the availability of grants.
4. Many governments are keen to promote the development of new businesses manufacturing, using and selling new technology.
5. A number of grants and schemes are aimed at specific groups of population: the disabled, the 'socially disadvantaged', ethnic minorities, the unemployed, etc.

Reducing your need to borrow

At the beginning of Chapter 7 you were encouraged to assess the financial needs of your business. Use this section to re examine these – can they be reduced, redrafted or reorganized to reduce the amount you need to borrow?

Premises

Rent rather than buy? Renting can greatly reduce capital outlay but at the same time it diminishes your capability to borrow further funds as little can be offered to the lender as security for the loan.

Equipment, machinery, fixtures and fittings, etc.

Rent, lease or buy second-hand? The disadvantage of renting is that operating costs can be higher, but will this be offset by not having to pay charges and interest on loans to acquire the item that would have to be otherwise pur chased. What are the benefits derived from releasing capital by this method for other purchases? Another factor to be considered is that rental and service agreements often offer service and maintenance. This helps you budget more easily this aspect of operating costs. If you are only going to use an item occasionally, can you hire it for short periods?

Stock

● Is your estimate for average stock level excessive?
● Can you adopt a different trading policy that involves a smaller range of goods to be carried without unduly harming sales potential?
● Can you obtain more frequent deliveries?
● Can you obtain stock on credit?
● Can you negotiate terms with suppliers where you only pay for the stock when you sell it (known as obtaining supplies on consignment)?

Debtors

● Can you increase your cash sales?
● Can you reduce the number of days' credit given to your customers?

Costs

● Have you re-examined all of your costs?
● Can any be reduced?
● Can you use self-employed labour instead of employing staff?
● Can you link wages to sales?
● Can payment of your overheads be spread over a greater period of time?

Still can't raise enough?

If after re-examination of the finance requirements you still cannot raise the necessary capital, then don't despair: calculate what scale of business the capital you can raise will support. A useful approach to this problem is to look again at the selling methods available to you. For instance, do you really need premises to sell from? Have you considered other methods of distribution (see Chapter 4)?

Presenting your case

The main reason why applications for business loans fail is that they are poorly researched and even more poorly presented. If you have researched and planned your business idea following the suggestions and techniques put forward in this book, you should not make this mistake. The most important thing to remember is that the lender sees the loan in terms of his/her organization making an investment in your business. They will, of course, want to know if their investment will be a profitable one for them. The key question in the forefront of their minds will be 'is there evidence of *ability to repay* the loan?' With a person who is employed, this is relatively easy to assess by referring to the applicant's job (i.e. how secure it is), salary and outgoings. With a business, in particular a new one without a proven track record, there is little solid evidence to prove the all-important ability to repay. This explains why a bank would rather lend £10 000 to an employed person with a relatively secure job to buy a car than lend the same amount to a person wishing to set up a new business. From the lender's point of view, one is relatively risk-free and the other fraught with risk. The lending organization must therefore be convinced of your business's ability to repay. The only way to do this is to prepare and present a *business plan*.

The business plan

The lender is likely to want satisfactory answers to the following, or similar, questions before granting the loan.

What is the business? Does it sound like a viable concern?

Information required:

● Brief summary of business idea.
● Basic information: business name, address, legal identity (e.g. sole trader, partnership, limited company) (see Chapter 9).
● Management of the business: brief and concise, e.g. key personnel, functions, etc.

● Nature of your proposed business. What marks it as different from your competitors? Essentially projecting to the potential lender 'what business you are in' (see Chapter 2) and why your product and service will sell (see Chapters 3 and 4).

Are you the right type of person to run this type of business?

Information required: summary of:

● Personal details.
● Relevant work experience, skills and education.

How much am I being asked to invest and for what?

Information required (see Chapter 7):

● Exact amount of money you want.
● Period you want to borrow it for.
● What exactly you are going to use it for – working capital, premises, fixtures and fittings, etc.

Does the business have a sufficient market for its product or service – will it be able to reach and exploit it?

Information required (see Chapters 3 and 4):

● Summary of the market segments with particular reference to expected revenue they will generate.
● Market share expected.
● Estimates of sales for each month in your first year.
● Estimates of sales for second year.
● How you will reach and sell to your markets.
● All projections and statements backed up with evidence of credible market research.

Will the business make a viable profit?

Information required (see Chapter 6):

● Details of costs and sales including timings.
● Projection of when the business will be earning profits.
● Break-even analysis, showing the effect on the business of best and worst expectations.
● Expected return on capital employed.

Is the proposed business properly financed – does it have sufficient capital?

Information required (see Chapter 7):

● Projected balance sheet for start of business. This will show how the capital invested in the business will be used. It will also show the lender your intended equity in the business; that is, how much of the net assets employed in the business you are going to finance from personal funds. Most banks will expect you to have at least a 50% holding in the business.

● Cash flow projection with explanatory notes. This is essential to show the lender your expected borrowing requirements over time. It demonstrates that the business will be able to remain solvent (i.e. be able 'to pay its way'). The cash flow should include repayments of the loan applied for – obviously essential as key evidence to the lending organization that you will be able to repay the loan.

● Details of the working capital required and how it will be financed.

● Evidence that you have allowed for unforeseen costs and capital requirements.

In addition, you will have to include details of the security and personal guarantees offered in case the business fails. The actual way you lay out your loan application (business plan) is up to you to decide as long as you make sure you satisfactorily answer the potential lender's key concerns. Many banks now produce their own guides to how you should lay out your business loan application – they are usually in the form of a checklist of questions. The simple advice is to make sure you answer them!

When compiling your business plan, adhere to the following guidelines:

1. Have it typed double-spaced with wide margins (this to allow the lender to make notes as he studies it).
2. The application should not be too long – try and go for a positive and concise presentation of the facts. Use diagrams and graphs where appropriate.
3. Adopt a layout that makes sense and is easy to understand. Prepare the application in sections, number

the paragraphs and pages so that you can easily refer the reader to relevant information, graphs and diagrams.

The complexity of the application will of course depend on the nature and scale of your business. If you find the task of compiling the report is beyond you, it is possible to pay for it to be produced. Obviously, you will still have to do the hard work of producing the information on which it is to be based!

Once completed, the application should be sent to or left at the lending organization's offices a week before the interview to allow the lender time to study it. At the actual interview, quite naturally you will be nervous, but try and project an air of confidence (however, don't 'go over the top'!). Be positive, don't evade questions, be frank (lenders with experience are not easily fooled) and above all don't waffle. Dress smartly but conservatively for the occasion and, very important, watch your body posture. Many of us have very irritating habits that we are only partly aware of, such as continually tapping on desks, slumping in chairs, leaning too far forward when talking, or looking anywhere but at a person when talking to them. Watch out for your bad habits. Remember, you have to sell yourself as well as your business.

Summary

Every business at some time in its life will require finance from external sources. You will need to know not just how much you need to borrow but also when. In choosing a finance package it is important to consider the type of finance in relation to the specific use it will be put to.
The key questions any lender will ask are: Is there ability to repay? Is there adequate security and does the applicant have sufficient equity in the business? The business plan is the crucial factor in any loan application.

9

before you start up, have you ...?

*The legal form of your business • Business names •
Protecting yourself and your business • Tax matters •
Other legal considerations • Before you start –
a checklist*

If you have used each chapter in this book to help you
research and plan your business venture, you will now be
nearly ready to 'start up'. However, there are still some
important considerations left, such as the legal form your
business should take, tax considerations and licences. You
should also take one last look at your business venture
before you start up. This is the purpose of this chapter, to tie
up loose ends and provide you with a general checklist
before taking the final step!

The legal form of your business

Legally, all businesses fall into one of the following main
categories:

- sole trader
- partnership
- limited company
- co-operative

Each has its own advantages and disadvantages. Your
choice depends on weighing up the pros and cons in relation
to your business's needs – there is no right answer. Your
accountant and solicitor should be able to advise and help
you come to a decision. What follows is a brief description
of each form and a summary of the main advantages and
disadvantages.

Sole trader

Setting up as a sole trader is perhaps the simplest way of entering into business. From a legal point of view, there is nothing you have to do to set up in business as a sole trader.

Advantages

1. Easy to set up – there are no legal formalities.
2. You have total control of the business.
3. You are taxed as an individual.
4. Accounts do not have to be disclosed to the public.
5. Easy to wind up.
6. Some tax advantages in the short term.

Disadvantages

1. You are totally responsible and liable for all business losses. If the business goes bankrupt, so do you. Your creditors will be entitled (through the courts) to seize your personal as well as business possessions.
2. Does not have the status of, say, a limited company.

Partnership

If two or more people go into business together without registering as a limited company or co-operative, they are forming a partnership. Again you can enter into business like this without any legal formalities. However, you would be ill-advised to enter into a partnership without a formal partnership agreement, even more so if you are entering with a relative or close friend. The main reasons for this are to prevent severe disagreements about how the business should be operated and, should the partnership be wound up or sold, how the proceeds should be distributed. Remember, all may seem rosy now but the best of friendships do not always last for ever, particularly when exposed to the stresses and strains of running a business. The partnership agreement is there to protect you, your friendship and the business.

Partnership agreements should cover the following as applicable:

● Who is responsible for what?
● How many hours should each partner devote to the business?

Starting your business

- When and for how long can each partner take his/her holidays?
- How much can each partner draw out of the business?
- Will cheques to be drawn on the business's bank account require more than one partner's signature?
- How are major decisions to be reached? One vote per partner, or otherwise?
- Will there be any system for settling disputes between partners?
- How are the profits to be divided?
- How long should the partnership last?
- How much notice should be given if one partner wants to withdraw?
- How will the proceeds of the business be split up if the partnership is dissolved?
- Will there be a provision for accepting new partners into the business?
- What happens if one partner dies? Will the partnership be automatically dissolved?

The list could almost be endless! There are obviously all kinds of eventualities to be considered. Some partnership agreements, because of the nature of the business, are simple; others more complex. What should be in your partnership agreement? Sit down with your partner(s) and work out the rough details and then go and see your solicitor for further advice.

Advantages

1. A good way of pooling complementary skills and knowledge.
2. A way of starting a business that requires more capital than you have at your disposal.
3. Can help share the work load and pressures associated with running a small business.
4. Other advantages similar to those of being a sole trader, except you are not totally responsible.

Disadvantages

1. Each partner is responsible for all business debts, even if incurred by another partner.
2. There are some legal costs involved in drawing up a

partnership agreement.

3. There is always a risk of personality clashes ruining the business.
4. The death or bankruptcy of any one partner, unless there are arrangements to the contrary, will automatically dissolve the partnership.
5. Can be difficult to expand the business by introducing new partners.

Limited company

The word 'limited' in this context means your liability to repay the business's debts is 'limited' to the amount you have agreed to contribute to them. Therefore, if the business goes bankrupt, your personal possessions cannot be seized to pay the company's debts. This is, as you can imagine, the greatest attraction of forming a business in this way. However, there are a number of disadvantages (see later). A limited company has a legal identity which is separate from its shareholders. Like an individual, the company itself can enter into contracts with other organizations and individuals, sue and be sued and prosecuted without involving its shareholders in the proceedings. Put simply, once a limited company is formed it exists in its own right and will remain in existence indefinitely, even if it ceases trading, until such time as action is taken to wind it up.

A limited company is formed with a minimum of two shareholders. A director must be appointed from the shareholders, and a company secretary appointed who can be an outsider. With a small business this is usually the business's accountant or solicitor. Further to this, a limited company prior to registration must produce, and later adhere to, two principal documents, the Memorandum and Articles of Association. These are complex documents but can be simply summarized as follows.

The Memorandum sets out the main objectives of the company. These are usually set quite wide to allow the company to sell or manufacture other products and services as it expands. The Memorandum details the company's share capital. The Articles of Association set out additional rules by which the company will be governed. In many ways it is similar in content, but not style, to some aspects of a partnership agreement. To the lay person, both documents can be incomprehensible as they tend to over-use legal jargon. However, most use standard phrases and therefore you will find that many Memorandums and Articles of Association are similar. As you can see, specialist advice from a solicitor is needed if you wish to form or 'buy' a limited company.

If you wish to have limited company status there are two options open to you. You can buy one 'off the shelf' or start one from scratch. Buying one 'off the shelf' means buying an existing company that has no assets and is not trading. These 'off the shelf' companies are offered by sale in the UK by specialist companies known as 'company registration agents'. They keep a stock of companies (that they have properly registered) suitable for a range of businesses. On 'transfer' of the company to its 'new owners' all that has to be done is for the existing shareholders (nominees of the company registration agent) to resign to allow the purchasers to become the new shareholders and appoint directors. Because there is less legal work to be done in buying a ready-made company, it is the cheapest method. However, the way you intend to establish your business may demand that you start a company from scratch. If this is the case, expensive legal work can increase the costs from hundreds to thousands of pounds!

If you form a limited company, you, as one of the directors, will have the following responsibilities:

● you will have to attend properly conducted board meetings
● you will have to disclose interests and shares in the company
● you must take reasonable steps to make sure you know what is going on in your company and act in a manner that is honest and diligent
● accordingly, if you allow the company to trade while knowing it can't meet its debts, you may well find yourself personally liable
● you may not borrow money from the company
● you cannot exceed the powers granted to you in the Articles of Association
● you must be elected by the shareholders and accordingly

you can be removed by them

Advantages of being a limited company

1. Limited liability.
2. Higher level of status/improved image.
3. Capital may be increased by selling shares.
4. You will be an employee of the company.
5. Management structure of the business is better defined.
6. The business is not affected if shareholders die or become bankrupt.
7. Disposal or acquisition of shares can easily be arranged.

Disadvantages

1. Limited liability status can for all intents and purposes be removed with the increasing practice of lending institutions asking for personal guarantees from directors and major shareholders.
2. Can be very costly to set up.
3. The business will have to make public its accounts, which means telling your competitors what your sales, costs, assets, liabilities were last year!
4. You will probably need continuing professional advice to meet your legal obligations as a limited company.
5. As an employee of the company you will be subject to PAYE.
6. You can only start trading after the company has been properly formed.

Co-operative

Forming a co-operative is only suitable for those people setting up in business with a strong wish to adhere to and practise democratic/collectivist principles. The main characteristics of a co-operative are as follows:

● The business is owned and controlled by those working in it.
● Membership is usually open to all employees, but sometimes subject to special conditions.
● Profits are not shared on the basis of the amount of capital put into the business by an individual. Rather, they are distributed in proportion with the amount of work done by each member.

Business names

If you intend to set up in business as a sole trader using your own name you will have no problems in this area. However, to project a better image to your market and suppliers you may wish to trade under a business name.

You cannot trade under any name you wish. There are certain names that you cannot use because they may imply that you are something which you are not. The Department of Trade produces a useful leaflet called *Business Names – Guidance Notes* which lists some 90 words such as 'royal' and 'authority' which you cannot use without official clearance.

If you trade under a business name, then you must display on your premises, letter-heads, invoices, sales receipts, etc. the following information:

- business name
- your name (and name of partners if a partnership, or full name of company in the case of a limited company)
- your permanent business address

When choosing a business name you should also take care that you do not take unfair advantage of a competitor by selecting a similar one and 'cashing in' on their reputation/goodwill or you could find yourself in court!

Protecting yourself and your business

Trade marks and patents

There are various methods of protecting your business from unfair competition. If your idea is original in some way and if you think it could be easily copied by a competitor you may consider investigating the possibility of applying for a patent or registering a trade mark. However, be warned: it can be a difficult and costly business proving that somebody has copied your idea. As a small business, could you afford the legal expenses? One good idea though is to check with the Trade Marks Registry that the logo or name you intend to use is not already registered by somebody who can afford legal action!

Insurance

You can insure almost anything against any eventuality if you are prepared to pay the price!

From a practical point of view, you should have adequate insurance to cover:

● *Public liability* – to cover legal liability for death, injury or illness to a member of the public caused by defects in your premises, products, services or by negligence by you or your employees.

● *Employer's liability* – this is similar to public liability and covers legal claims by your employees. You are forced to carry this cover by law.

● *Professional liability* – applicable to businesses such as management consultants who may unwittingly or negligently give wrong advice to a client.

● *Personal accident insurance* – should be taken out to cover your future financial security in the event of a disabling illness or accident. You may also wish to take out additional cover for employees engaged in potentially dangerous work.

● *Goods in transit* – applicable to businesses who despatch expensive goods to customers. The goods will be your risk until they reach the customer.

● *Bad debts* – the premiums can be expensive but worthwhile if a large proportion of your credit sales are with a few customers. What would happen to your business if one of them went bankrupt?

● *Fire, flood, storm, water damage, consequential loss of profits, commercial use of motor cars* – are all your assets, from premises to cash, properly covered? Remember, if your business is closed down for a month due to, say, fire damage your overheads will still mount up and profits from sales will be lost. Will you be covered for this?

Don't forget to shop around for the best deal on price, payment terms and quality of cover.

Tax matters

Income tax

The two things you would be well advised to do before starting in business are:

1. Employ the services of a good accountant. This does not mean that you should not keep your own books but, rather, dealing with the Inland Revenue is in many cases best left to the professional. At the very least you will need advice from your accountant on the best kind of bookkeeping system to use, choice of accounting date (the date when you draw up your final accounts) and the tax rules governing what you can and cannot offset against tax.

2. Inform your local Inland Revenue offices of the date you intend to commence trading. This, if nothing else, gets your relationship with the Inland Revenue off to a good start They will also supply you with a booklet entitled *Starting in Business* giving you an overview of taxation and the self-employed.

As previously noted, if you start in business as a sole trader or partnership you will be taxed on your net profits as shown in your profit and loss account. However, it is possible that the Inland Revenue will slightly adjust the net profit figure because of special rules they apply to the calculation of depreciation on certain assets for tax purposes. Your accountant will advise you of the details and make the necessary adjustments if required. As for the rate of tax you are charged and your tax coding (personal allowances), there is no difference between self-employment and employment.

Besides the nature of the allowances you can claim, the main difference between employment and self-employment for tax purposes is the time period of the earnings/profits on which your tax is based and the payment dates. As you will be aware, as an employed person your tax is calculated on your weekly or monthly earnings. As a self-employed person the rules are different and quite complicated. You should appreciate that when you first start trading no accurate assessment of your earnings can be made until after you have drawn up your first final accounts some 12 months later. The first thing to note is that you will not have to pay any tax until some 14 to 18 months or more after starting up.

It is beyond the scope of this book to deal with the full complexities of taxation.

Value Added Tax

Many references have already been made to VAT in earlier chapters. First, you should note that an informative and comprehensive pack of free material is available from your local VAT office (look up the number in your telephone directory).

To the newcomer, VAT can appear a horribly complicated tax, but in essence the principle is quite straightforward; it is the paperwork that goes with it that is laborious and sometimes complex. It is in actual fact a tax on the value you add to goods and services, which is payable by the end purchaser.

Let's take a simple example to demonstrate the process. Take the case of a retailer buying and selling goods on which VAT is payable at 17.5%. Let's imagine the retailer buys goods from a wholesaler at a VAT-exclusive cost of £100. He will actually pay £117.50 (cost price plus 17.5% VAT). Now let's assume he sells all those goods at a markup of 100% (profit margin of 50%). He will receive £200 plus 17.5% VAT on the selling prices, a total of £235. The VAT he paid is known as his *input tax* and is reclaimable; the VAT he charged on the sales, which is known as his *output tax*, is payable to the Customs & Excise. The VAT actually due is the difference between his output tax of £35 (VAT on sales) and his input tax of £17.50 (VAT on cost of goods), a total of £17.50; which is exactly 17.5% of £100, the value added to the goods! In theory, the existence of VAT does not affect the profits. If VAT didn't exist, the gross profit would be: £200 (selling price) – £100 (cost price) = £100. With the existence of VAT the same is true, £235 (amount actually received from sales) – £117.50 (amount actually paid for stock) = £117.50 (the amount held before payment of VAT) – £17.50 (VAT payable) = £100 gross profit. You should be able to see that it is the customer who actually pays the VAT on the value you added to the stock and it is you who has collected the tax on behalf of the Customs & Excise! The existence of VAT, through forcing the consumer to incur extra expenditure, indirectly reduces overall sales and therefore profits.

The following are important points to note about VAT:

1. You must be registered for VAT if you expect your sales of applicable items to exceed the VAT threshold in any quarter or 12-month period.
2. It is your responsibility to register for VAT. It is no excuse to say you did not realize your turnover would be 'that large': the Customs & Excise will still demand the VAT due even if you haven't charged it.
3. The Customs & Excise have wide-ranging powers of search and entry. Any attempt to defraud them can easily lead to a prison sentence
4. You will need proof of all your inputs and outputs.
5. If you are not sure about any aspect of VAT in relation to your business, contact your local VAT office before you make a complete mess of things. They will only be too pleased to help as it is within their interests for you to get it right at the outset!
6. In some instances it can actually be beneficial for a business to be registered because VAT paid on some capital items can be recovered.

Other legal considerations

Licences

Registration, permission or a licence is required under the law for some business activities; for others it may be desirable but not legally necessary. If your business will involve any of the following activities, then you certainly would be recommended to seek legal advice:

- nursing care
- employing or care of children
- credit and loan activities
- gambling
- employment agencies
- change of use of premises

Many other activities such as door-to-door selling, taxi licences, food and catering are covered by local and national government legislation and bodies. In all cases you should consult and check with the following to see if any permission, licences or registration are required.

- planning department
- environmental health
- Trading Standards Office
- police
- Clerk to the Justices (licensed premises).

If you are still unsure, check with your solicitor.

Consumer legislation

There are comprehensive laws in existence to protect the rights of the consumer. You should make sure that your trading policy adheres to them. Otherwise, two serious consequences might result:

1. Prosecution.
2. Loss of reputation and customer goodwill, particularly if the incident is reported in the local press.

Contact your local Trading Standards Office who will provide you with useful free booklets and further advice if you need it.

The main pieces of legislation that concern most businesses are the Consumer Protection Act, the Sale of Goods and Services Act, the Trade Descriptions Act, the Weights and Measures Act, the Consumer Safety Act, the Consumer Credit Act and the Food Hygiene Regulations. These collectively make it an offence to sell or manufacture goods that are unfit for human consumption, not correctly described, unsafe, of incorrect measure, unfit for the purpose for which they were sold and not of merchantable quality (not to generally accepted standards).

It is very important that you find out and adhere to the legislation that affects your particular business. You will get all the advice you need on this subject from the appropriate department of your local authority – make use of it! Many traders don't and still display illegal signs such as 'No refunds given', make false statements, sell goods that have passed their 'sell by' date, produce misleading advertisements, etc. What such illegal actions are doing to their sales is incalculable and in any case it is just a matter of time before they end up in court!

Contracts

Every time you buy or sell something, either in business or in your private life, you enter into a contract, which can be written, verbal or both. A contract exists as soon as an offer to sell or buy is made and accepted by both parties. Any statement made about the goods and services pertinent to the transaction during the course of the sale becomes part of the terms of the contract. If either of the parties to the contract feels that the terms have been broken, then they can attempt to settle the matter by civil action in the courts. It is therefore advisable that your general terms of trade are vetted by a solicitor before you commence business and that they appear on all the necessary purchase and sales documentation that you plan to use.

For much more detailed guidance and discussion on business law, consult *Law for Small Businesses* in the NatWest Business Handbook series.

Employment legislation

Employees have comprehensive rights under various Acts of Parliament. However, businesses which only employ a few people or part-timers are exempt from some of the regulations. It is outside the scope of this book to deal with the complex subject of employment legislation. A range of free booklets on all aspects of employing staff are available from the Advisory Conciliation and Arbitration Service (ACAS), Clifton House, 83-118 Euston Road, London NE1 2RB. Tel.: 0171 388 5100.

Before you start – a checklist

The following is a broad checklist to help you, as far as possible, to check that you have considered and done all the necessary research and planning before taking the final few steps to starting your business. Some reminders will not be appropriate for the smaller, simpler business whereas for the more complex operation there is not enough detail here. You may find it a valuable exercise to draw up your own final planning list and certainly a time schedule of the things that have to be done in the last few weeks before you actually open your doors to custom. You will have enough to do then without trying to solve any unforeseen problems and chasing up things you should have done weeks ago.

	Done	Require more action	When

You and your business

● Have you selected a business idea that will suit your personality, aptitude, skills and commitments?

● Have you identified your strengths and weaknesses in relation to running your business?

● Have you considered and obtained personal insurance to cover accident and sickness?

● Have you drawn up contingency plans to operate the business if you should become ill or suffer an accident?

The market and sales

● Have you established what the principal selling points of your business will be?

● Do you know why customers will buy your products?

● Have you identified your market segment(s) and detailed their characteristics including their needs, purchasing power and buying behaviour?

● Have you estimated your market share?

● Have you produced projected sales figures over your first year's trading?

● Do you know the threats and opportunities your competition presents?

	Done	Require more action	When
● Have you decided on how you will distribute (or sell) your product?			
● Have you fully developed sales promotion to implement at start-up?			
● Have you developed a trading policy?			
● Do you know how sensitive your sales will be to fluctuation in price?			
● Are all your findings about your markets supported by valid and reliable market research?			

Costs

● Have you anticipated all the costs?			
● Have you allowed for unforeseen costs?			
● Do you know when you will incur these costs?			
● Have you calculated break-even points for various fluctuations in overheads and variable costs?			

Profit

● Have you produced profit forecasts?			
● Have you established your target profits?			
● Do you know how sensitive your profit is to changes in sales volume, price and costs?			
● Have you built a margin of safety into all your forecasts?			
● Have you projected a rate of return your business will give your capital employed?			

	Done	Require more action	When

Working capital

● Have you calculated how much working capital your business will require on average?

● Have you explored ways of reducing the net working capital required?

● Have you calculated how much working capital will be required to start the business?

● Have you compiled a cash flow forecast for your first 12 months?

● Is it based on well-researched facts?

● Have you taken all possible steps to minimize cash flow problems?

Fixed assets

● Have you made a detailed checklist to select major fixed assets, say based on quality, price, reliability, suitability, etc. ...?

● Have you a detailed list of requirements?

● Have you researched the alternatives of leasing, renting or buying second-hand?

● Have you checked availability?

Premises

● Have you fully researched the location and assessed its suitability for your business?

● Have you obtained the necessary legal advice?

● Do you have security of tenure?

	Done	*Require more action*	*When*

● Do you have the necessary
planning permission?

● Have you taken into account
future space requirements?

● Have you calculated all the
costs involved in the purchase or
acquisition?

Staff

● Have you checked out the
availability of suitable staff?

● Have you calculated the full
costs of employing staff, including
management and administration
training recruitment and selection
National Insurance contributions
employee facilities industrial
relations/disputes?

● Have you considered the criteria
you will use to select staff?

● Have you thought out systems
to train and motivate them?

● Do you understand your main
responsibilities to staff as laid out
by the Employment and Health and
Safety at Work laws?

● Have you obtained employees'
liability insurance cover?

Finance

● Have you calculated how much
you will need, when and for what?

● Have you attempted to match
the right finance to the right use?

● Have you completed your
business plan/loan proposals?

● Have you had initial discussions
with your bank?

	Done	Require more action	When
● Do you know from your cash flow the size of overdraft facility you will need?			
● Have you discussed this with your bank?			
● Have you checked the availability of grants?			

Tax and legal

● Have you decided on the legal form of your business?			
● If a partnership, have you had a partnership agreement drawn up and signed?			
● Have you sought legal advice – have you selected a solicitor?			
● Are you aware of the legal controls and restrictions on your business?			
● Does your trading policy or manufacturing process take these legal controls into consideration?			
● Have you checked whether you should obtain a licence, planning permission or register your business in some way?			
● Have you checked whether you should be registered for VAT?			
● Have you informed the Inland Revenue when you intend to commence trading?			
● Have you made arrangements for payment of class 2 National Insurance contributions?			
● Have you made plans to cover insurable eventualities?			

	Done	*Require more action*	*When*

Business control and administration

● Have you chosen a bookkeeping system?

● Do you know how to use it?

● Have you selected an accountant?

● Have you taken action to guard against theft?

● Have you a stock control system?

● Have you opened a business bank account?

● Do you have a system to control cash?

● Do you have a system to monitor and control debtors?

● Do you have a system to monitor sales, identify fast and slow sellers?

● Have you identified suppliers of stock including their terms and delivery capabilities?

● Do you have a system to monitor profits?

● Have you drawn up plans to organize the work load for yourself and your staff?

● Have you had the necessary business documentation printed?

● Have you considered in advance how you will tackle routine problems?

● Have you put together a time schedule, complete with all the major things you will need to do over the weeks before commencement of trading?

Finally, good luck!

index

Index